A TRIBUTE
to
Moms

My mother planted seeds of faith

and watered them with love

Ruth Senter & Jori Senter Stuart

MULTNOMAH BOOKS   SISTERS, OREGON

A TRIBUTE TO MOMS

published by Multnomah Books
a part of the Questar publishing family

© 1997 by Ruth Senter and Jori Senter Stuart

International Standard Book Number: 1-57673-133-2

Cover photo by xxx

Designed by Kevin Keller

Printed in the United States of America

Most Scripture quotations are from the *New International Version* (NIV)
© 1973, 1984 by International Bible Society
used by permission of Zondervan Publishing House

Also quoted:

The *The Holy Bible, New Century Version* (NCV)
© 1991 Word Publishing

For information:
QUESTAR PUBLISHERS, INC.
POST OFFICE BOX 1720
SISTERS, OREGON 97759

Library of Congress Cataloging-in-Publication Data
Senter, Ruth Hollinger, 1944– A tribute to moms/Ruth Senter, Jori Senter Stuart.
p.cm. ISBN 1-57673-133-2 (alk. paper)
1. Mothers and daughters. 2. Mothers and daughters—Religious aspects. 3. Parent and adult child—Religious aspects.
I. Stuart, Jori Senter. II. Title HQ755.86.S46 1997 96-6712 306.874'3—dc21 CIP

97 98 99 00 01 02 03 04 05 — 10 9 8 7 6 5 4 3 2 1

To my mother, Gertrude Hollinger,

who lives the joy of mothering.

Ruth Senter

To my grandma, Gertrude Hollinger,

who is a living testimony to Psalm 103:17—

"But the Lord's love for those who respect Him

will continue forever and ever,

and His goodness continues to their grandchildren" (NCV).

To my mom, Ruth Senter. There is no way I can describe,

in a few words, a short chapter or even volumes of books,

all that you mean to me. You are my hero.

And to my sister-in-law, Cheryl Osborne,

who exemplifies everything I hope one day to be as a mother.

Philipians 1:3—"I thank my God every time I remember you."

Jori Senter Stuart

ACKNOWLEDGEMENTS

*I*t was a crisp, Chicago spring day when my mother and I first came up with the idea for this book. I was visiting my parents; they proudly showed me the first "empty nest" house they had bought. The papers were not yet signed, but a moving day was set.

Today the air is cool in London, Ontario, where I live. The leaves are starting to fall from the trees. Tomorrow I head back to Chicago to visit my parents, this time in their new house. This book was born, nurtured, and polished during these months of transition, amidst moving boxes and general household upheaval. That is how much my mother and I believed in our idea.

We are grateful to the folks at Multnomah Books who first believed in our project. How remarkable that when we came to them with our idea we learned they'd had the same idea. Special thanks to Alice Gray for her encouragement and assistance.

A big "thank you" also to all the authors who contributed to this book. They have been a delight to work with—everyone of them. These authors are some of the busiest women we know, and yet they willingly took time to contribute to our project.

From the moment of conception, we received overwhelming support and encouragement from the folks I work with at Beacon Distributing. Special thanks to Warren Benson, Don Pape, Sandy Ryerse, Tina Henwood, Rebecca Clark, and the "Beacon Boys"—Merv McKinney, Phil Maloney and Clint Steenson. (Thanks also to Gisele Budgell who spent a morning chasing down five lost chapters!!)

To our loyal cheerleader and prayer warrior, Kim Wilson, our heartfelt thanks.

Of course, we could not have done any of this without the support and encouragement of our husbands—Mark Senter and Ross Stuart—who have put up with an endless stream of faxes and e-mail, not to mention hours of phone calls! We love you both.

Our prayer is that this book will honor mothers everywhere, and glorify the One who created motherhood. Our deepest appreciation is to Him.

—*Jori Senter Stuart*

CONTENTS

CHAPTER ONE

STORIES IN THE DARK
by Gloria Gaither

*M*other was a renegade, always wild and free even though, as a minister's wife, she lived in a very structured framework.

Growing up, I always had the feeling that Mother belonged with us kids more than she belonged in the adult world. Oh, she was classy and could function with grace in sophisticated circles, but I always felt that she was in secret conspiracy with us, that when grownups' backs were turned, she really became one of us again.

My sister and I once had a pajama party. It was late when Mother called upstairs in her sternest voice, "You girls go to sleep now. It's too late for any more nonsense." Knowing that she usually meant what she said, we had all snuggled down and begun to doze when someone felt water drops on her bed. We began to stir again and whisper to one another. Soon, we felt more water drops. Finally, someone got up and tiptoed to the open window. There was Mother, standing in the backyard in her nightgown, spraying us with the garden hose through the second story window. We burst into giggles and ran downstairs, only to find a great dishpan full of fresh popcorn waiting for us in the kitchen. We all sat in a circle on the kitchen floor in the dark as Mother told us stories she remembered from her childhood in the Ozarks.

Yes, Mother taught me how to laugh—sometimes at life, sometimes at myself. She always saw the funny things in life, and she made sure I saw them, too.

Although we never had much money, I was not aware of being poor. Indeed, I *wasn't* poor. Mother clothed me extravagantly with her creativity, decorated our home with a designer's flair, and filled our lives with activities that drew friends like flies. Our home pulsated with life, and of all the good things, there was more than enough.

Mother was a fighter. She was strong in will and character, absolutely fearless in the face of evil when she was convinced that right was on her side. I think she would have taken on any army of devils, but she also had a healthy respect for Satan as a living entity; she never allowed us to make light of his reality or to toy with spiritism. Yet, she taught us that even the weakest believer has power over all the forces of hell when we speak and claim the name of Jesus.

She was just as fearless in the face of daily obstacles. I never remember her saying, "I can't" or "I don't know how." When something needed to be done, she assumed that there was a way to do it. And if there was a way, she would find it. She had little patience with complainers and a firm belief in ingenuity and plain old hard work.

Mother never considered herself merely "the minister's wife," but a minister herself, accountable to God for her calling. She felt that any minister's wife would fail and eventually drag her husband down with her unless she felt a deep personal responsibility for serving God with what he'd given her. Only then, she believed, could she handle all the pressures the parsonage life would bring.

Mother was a confronter. I knew I couldn't con her or avoid her. She had eyes in the back of her head, but those eyes were not just for seeing my failures and mistakes. They were more often for seeing some spark of genius, some glimmer of beauty, some splash of creativity. She always caught me when I did something sneaky, but she caught me, too, when I did things right. She didn't brag on me or condemn me. Instead, she let me know what I was exemplifying or failing to live up to—what she knew I was capable of, holding up my best achievement as a standard for myself.

During my adolescence, she often assured me that she trusted me implicitly but that she did not always trust the changes in my body chemistry and my mercuric emotions at that time of my life. I felt that she was on my side, encouraging me and wanting the best and highest in me to win out.

Often she reminded me that if I found myself in an uncomfortable situation, I could always call home; that avoiding a trap was a courageous and intelligent thing to do. Most of all, she kept me aware of the Holy Spirit's presence in my life to give wisdom and directions when I couldn't see clearly.

I truly believe that the commandment for children to obey their parents does not end when the child turns eighteen years old, or when she gets married, or even when the parent dies. I find myself even now seeking wisdom from my mother's words, gleaning from her poetry and prose, and working the principles she taught me into the fabric of my own life.

Recently, as I went to check the spelling of a word, I reread a poem my mother wrote on the inside cover of the dictionary I was awarded for winning a speech contest in high school:

The sheep may know the pasture
But the Shepherd knows the sheep;
The sheep lie down in comfort,
But the Shepherd does not sleep.

He protects the young and foolish,
From their unprecocious ways,
And gently prods the aged,
Lest they give in to the day.

When the young have learned some wisdom,
it is much too late to act;
When the old man knows the method,
He is less sure of the fact.
Ah, the Shepherd knows the answer—
The beginning and the end.
So the wisest choice, my daughter,
Is to take him as your friend.
                    —Dorothy Sickal

Gloria Gaither is an author, lyricist, teacher, speaker, mother, and grandmother. She has authored twelve books, including *Hands Across the Seasons*[1], and the best-selling *What My Parents Did Right* and *Let's Make a Memory*. As a musician she has written lyrics to more than 600 songs, has recorded more that sixty albums, and is winner of the Dove Award. She has three children and three grandchildren. Gloria's mother, Dorothy Sickal, was a writer, artist and speaker who co-ministered with her husband for many years.

[1] Although *Hands Across the Seasons* is no longer in print, it can be purchased by contacting Gaither Family Resources, P. O. Box 737, Alexandria, IN 46001 or 800-955-8746.

CHAPTER TWO

DAILY REMINDERS OF MOTHER
by Elisabeth Elliot

*M*other used to remind us, "There are some things you will have to do all your life. Making your bed is one of them. So you might as well get used to doing it as quickly and neatly as possible."

So I have gotten up every day of my life, made my bed as quickly and efficiently as possible, and then proceeded with the rest of the day's work. How thankful all of her children are that Mother taught us simple principles which uncomplicate our lives today.

Mother came from a fairly well-to-do Philadelphia family. My father was from a family of more modest means. It was a new experience for both to live in a fourth-floor walk-up apartment in Belgium where they were missionaries for five years. Never did I hear Mother complain about having less than she had been used to having. She received thankfully what was given. She made no fuss about what was not given.

I'm quite sure she never thought of herself as terribly "spiritual," although she prayed with each of her children, taught the Bible, and spent quiet time alone with the Lord each morning.

Mother was a true woman. She dressed with taste and femininity, setting an example of unassuming grace for my sister and me.

She was the ace of efficiency and a whiz at housework, accomplishing things quickly and quietly and in an orderly fashion. I do not remember her ever raising her voice at any one of the six of us. There was a calm thoughtfulness and care about the way she did things, even down to wringing out the washcloths and hanging up the towels. There was a place for everything, and everything in its place. If something wasn't where it belonged, one of us was to blame and was called to account for it. Home was a place of peace—both parents teaching us by example to do things decently and in order, just as the Bible says.

As I work through my day at the age of seventy, I find that I still do things pretty much as I saw my mother do them. I often think, "This is my mother in me." Everything from how I dress and organize my work day, to how I wring out my washcloth and dry my toothbrush, to how I hang the laundry outdoors on the line and keep my dresser drawers organized reveals my wonderful mother's influence.

The older I get, the more I realize my debt to her.

Mother was gentle but firm. Her discipline started while we were still in the crib. She was convinced that a tiny infant learned early to respond to the gentle touch of a mother's hand and the loving tone of her voice. As we were growing up, there was an eighteen-inch switch placed over the door in every room. My mother had only to raise her eyes to that door and we straightened up. Spankings were few. We knew she meant what she said—the first time.

Mother enjoyed life. She often laughed until she cried. She was a great lover of books and began reading to us children early. Evenings often found all of us, except perhaps the youngest ones, sitting in the living room, each with a book. Sometimes our parents would read aloud to all of us, so it is not surprising that we are all book-lovers today.

In addition to three meals a day for the body, our family had two meals a day for the soul—one after breakfast and one after supper. Family worship included hymns, Bible reading, and prayer.

Often, Mother could be found sitting at the bay window in her bedroom on a small armless rocking chair, reading her Bible, singing softly, and sometimes writing in a little red notebook. She was a woman of The Word. From it she drew her quiet strength. Only once as a child did I see her cry—when I was six and Daddy left for a trip to the Holy Land. I found her on the porch blotting the tears, not wanting to upset any of us. I was awed by the sight but could think of nothing to say. As each of us grew up and went off to a far corner of the earth, it was a dreadful wrench for her but she did not try to clutch us to herself. She gave us to God, having learned, as she said, to hold all that she loved "on an open palm."

What do I value most about the legacy my mother left me? That is a very hard question. There was so much I wish I had learned far sooner, but in my old age I mainly thank God for her humility and simplicity. She was utterly unpretentious. She assumed no airs. I think it is quite true (though this would surprise her, I'm sure) to say that her attitude was much like that of Mary: "Behold the handmaiden of the Lord. Be it unto me according to Thy word."

Elisabeth Elliot served as a missionary to the Colorado, Quichua, and Auca Indians in South America for eleven years. She is the author of *Through Gates of Splendor*, the account of the 1956 death of her husband, Jim Elliot, and four other American missionaries in the Ecuadorian jungles. Her other books include *The Shaping of a Christian Family*, *Passion and Purity*, and its sequel, *Quest for Love*. Today she and her husband, Lars Gren, live on the coast of Massachusetts where she writes and conducts her radio broadcast, *Gateway to Joy*. Her father, Philip E. Howard, Jr., was editor of *The Sunday School Times*, a weekly magazine. Her mother, Katharine Gilingham, saw the raising of six children as God's very gracious gift.

CHAPTER THREE

SPRING-LOADED FOR FUN
by Colleen Townsend Evans

Her name was Stella. She was young and exceedingly attractive when her husband left her—and their baby—and never returned. It was rough going. The Depression was at its height. Jobs were scarce, and even if her husband had been gainfully employed—which at the time he was not—it is doubtful Stella would have sought alimony or even child support. She was that hurt, that proud, and that determined to make it on her own.

With only a few office skills and her high school diploma in hand, she felt fortunate to land a job in an insurance office where she worked from eight to five, five days a week, plus a half-day on Saturday—for $25.00 a week. It was hardly a good schedule for a woman totally committed to being a loving and responsible single parent, but that's the way it was and somehow she made it work. I know, because Stella was my mother.

Those were difficult years for most Americans. Families had to pull together, and that's what we did. In order to manage financially, we moved in with my mother's elderly and widowed father. He provided the house and she made the house a home. Every morning she left for work at seven, and got home at six. Her evenings were spent doing what most women did during the day, and she did it all on a budget that would challenge even the most frugal homemaker.

Looking back, I realize how difficult those early years must have been for her and how hard she had to work to provide a simple home for the three of us. We were poor by the world's standards, but I didn't know it. She didn't dwell on the sacrifices she was obviously making for me, so I didn't grow up feeling guilty.

My mother and I were such pals. It seemed to me that we had more fun together than many of my friends had with both of their parents. That was one of the many things my mother did right. In the midst of the daily struggle simply to survive and the very real pain she experienced over her broken marriage, she managed to have fun and to be fun. She did not allow the grim circumstances of her life to turn her into a grim person.

How did she do it? What did she do that was fun? She didn't do anything, really. She was too busy doing all she had to do. There was neither time nor money for special events, parties, gifts, or vacations. It was not what she did; it was who she was.

"Stella is so much fun," her friends would say—and that was it. She was not at all a Pollyanna. She was practical, realistic, and quick to speak her mind and to call a spade a spade. She carried a heavy load of responsibility which she took very seriously. But she was a woman anointed with gladness, spring-loaded for fun, ready in an instant to give a wink, pull a prank, or dance a jig. And that was a real gift to me. In fact, rather than feeling deprived as the only child of a single parent, I felt enriched because Stella was such a special person.

There was another thing my mother did right. She trusted me. I was still young when my grandfather, whom I loved dearly, died. That meant my mother had to leave me from early morning until six at night while she was at work. I was old enough to get myself to school on time and home again, but there were many hours every day when I was on my own.

My mother was a model of moral and ethical standards—both in principle and in practice—and she shared those convictions with me. She laid down guidelines and boundaries for me, but again it was not what she did in a structured way as much as who she was that really made the difference. Her attitude toward me was always one of trust. She *had* to trust me, and so she did.

Years later, when I was grown and had children of my own, my mother shared with me the struggle she had during those years when, against her every instinct, she left me alone day after day. Apparently, she often spent her hour-long morning bus ride to the office holding back tears and praying. Although she was not particularly religious, she had a deeply spiritual dimension, and she would fervently ask God to keep me from harm. She prayed for God to nurture within me a character worthy of trust. With wavering voice, my normally unemotional mother confessed to those being the most agonizing years of her life. But her trust in God and in her daughter brought her through. And through all the years of our life together, trust was the core of our relationship.

When I was fourteen and a Hollywood film contract beckoned, my mother neither pushed me nor held me back. She said, in essence, "It's your decision, honey. If it is what you want, Hollywood won't change you. I know you. I trust you." Years later, when I came to faith in Christ, my life was radically redirected and everything began to change. Again, her response was one of trust: "I don't quite understand it all, dear. But I see how much it means to you, so it must be right." And still later when I left my career to go where I sensed God was leading, she made no attempt to talk me out of that decision either. While other people around me lamented the financial and professional "sacrifice" I would be making, my mother was unwavering in her confidence and support: "I only want what is right for you, for your happiness. If you think this is what God wants of you, do it. I am with you all the way." At each crossroad, my mother said, "I trust you."

Through the years, my mother's spiritual heart and simple belief in God became a true faith and trust in Jesus Christ. She joined and was active in a church, and you might even say she became a little "religious." But consistent with her God-given personality, it was not so much what she said that made her so; it was who she was and how she lived.

My mother's willingness to trust me has given me an incredible gift. God used my mother and that trust to give me a sense of security and the desire to give our children the same depth of commitment and trust in them that my mother gave to me. But that isn't all. God also used my mother to teach me to have fun—not as a separate event but as an integral part of all the work, the responsibility, and even the agonies of parenting.

As if to remind me, my mother acted it out one day, in a memorable scene.

Louis and I and our four children had stopped by her house for a visit. After we had enjoyed one of her incredible meals, she walked with us to the car. As we said our hasty good-byes and fastened our seat belts, she stood by the curb, lifted her tailored skirt above her knees and did a fancy little jig. Our teenaged children, who absolutely loved their Grandmother Mimi, roared with laughter. As we pulled away from the curb, my mother, still dancing her jig, called, "Hey, hey! Not bad for an old girl, eh?" That's the last memory my children have of their grandmother on this earth. Not bad, Mom...indeed, not bad at all.

Colleen Townsend Evans is a mother, pastor's wife, author, and organizer. She and her husband, Louis H. Evans, Jr., minister at Menlo Park Presbyterian Church in Menlo Park, California. She has authored several books, including *A Deeper Joy, Teaching Your Child to Pray,* and *Vine Life.* Colleen is a board member for both Presbyterians for Renewal and World Vision U.S., and she served as chair for the Greater Washington Billy Graham Crusade. Colleen and her mother, Stella Townsend Wilholm, greatly enjoyed being with each other. When Colleen wasn't running a family or a ministry, writing, or working on community projects, and when her mother wasn't working at the insurance company, or any other time their schedules would permit, they spent time out of doors on picnics or on walks.

(Reprinted from, *What My Parents Did Right,* by Gloria Gaither. Used with permission.)

CHAPTER FOUR

THE RED LINOLEUM
by Margaret Jensen

I was going with Papa on a missionary journey!

Mama had packed the box on my lap and with tearful good-byes she waved. Papa cranked up the Model T.

We were off to Birch Hills, Saskatchewan, where Papa pitched a tent.

"Pay attention, Margaret!"

I did!

The farmers stood with hats in their rough hands to ask God's blessing on the tent meetings. The tent stakes were driven into the ground as Papa announced that someday there would be a church with a steeple rising to the sky!

I listened!

Years later, I realized that not only iron stakes were driven into the soil, but the faithful ones had driven the stakes of their faith into the fabric of the community, and I witnessed four generations of godly people worshipping in a beautiful church.

That was also the summer that I fell in love with the farmer's son. I was twelve.

I never saw him again because Papa got a "call" to Chicago.

With great excitement he waved the letter. "Mama, Mama look— Chicago!"

Papa loved Chicago, the windy city where he attended the Chicago University. He was a part of the noise and throbbing of a big city. Cows, chickens, manure, planting, and reaping had been a part of his early life—but it was the city that held him.

Mama loved the prairie!

She held the letter from the Logan Square First Norwegian Baptist Church.

"No, this cannot be God's will!"

I was sure thunder would roll from heaven. No one defied Papa!

"Why?" Papa looked at Mama in disbelief.

"Because God would never expect me to give up my red linoleum. It took a long time to save one dollar. God would never expect me to give up my prized possession."

I later realized that the red linoleum was indeed a prized possession. It covered the crack where the wind could blow—also the splinter that made scrubbing a hazard. It was also beauty in a small house, cheerful and warm on a cold winter night. It would blend with the polished stove and white starched curtains that framed sparkling windows. (Mama even had starched curtains in the outhouse.)

It was a thing of beauty when we sat by Mama in the rocking chair while we dipped a sugar lump in Mama's coffee and heard the songs she sang and stories she told.

It truly was a prized possession.

Papa was quiet. He didn't laugh at "foolishness." He knew Mama.

"Ja," he said. "We must pray."

"Ja," answered Mama. "I will put out the fleece. If someone comes to buy this little house without a sign, and then offers one dollar for the linoleum—then I will know God has spoken."

"Ja, Mama—so we pray!"

Papa was happy. He was sure God would send Gabriel to get Mama straightened out.

Mama was sure no one would buy a house without a "For Sale" sign. Mama loved the wind on the prairie. This was their own home— a garden—and red linoleum. She felt blessed.

One day a woman stopped to talk with Mama as she tended her garden.

"Oh my, what a cute house!"

"Oh Ja, it is cozy."

"I'm looking for a little house like this—would you sell it?"

"Oh, no!"

Then Mama remembered.

"Come inside and we'll have a cup of coffee."

While Mama put on the coffee pot, the woman noticed the red linoleum.

"Ja," Mama said, "it is beautiful. I paid a whole dollar for it."

So, it came to pass that Papa rejoiced, Mama was terrified of the gangsters in Chicago and her five children pressed their noses against the sooty windows to watch their world go by—never to return to the prairies again.

Mama said, "When God has spoken—don't look back."

She didn't know that when she gave up the red linoleum the day would come when she would have wall-to-wall carpet. She didn't know that when she left the scrub board and washtub behind the day would come when she would have a washer and dryer.

When we yield what is our prized possession, God will restore in His time, in His own way.

Mama said, "Don't look back." But, I'm looking back and I see God's faithfulness to each generation.

Seven children and their mates rise up and call Mama "blessed."

Margaret Jensen is a storyteller, first and foremost. It was from her mother that she learned many of the stories she has written in her eleven books, the most recent being *All God's Children Got Robes*, published by Multnomah Books. She has an extensive speaking ministry that takes her across the United States, Canada, and Europe. Margaret's mother, Ella Tweten, was a missionary and pastor's wife who lived out the gift of hospitality and unconditional love.

CHAPTER FIVE

MASTERFUL STORYTELLER
by Karen Dockrey

*M*y "mama" loves to tell this story.

Bill and Alan were playing the board game with the intense competition for which siblings are famous. It looked close for a while. But Bill, as usual, won.

Even after the game ended, the rivalry continued.

"You put the game away since I got it out," Bill said.

"No, you put it away!" countered Alan.

Alan bounded up the stairs to make sure he didn't get caught packing up the game. Bill was right behind him.

"No, I got it out so you have to put it away!" Bill insisted. He caught Alan mid-flight and pitched him back down the stairs.

"Owwwww!!" Alan yelled, landing full force on his foot. "You hurt my foot!"

"You just don't want to put the game away," challenged Bill. All the rest of the day, Alan limped.

My mama thought he was just after sympathy and not seriously injured.

That evening, when she found him lying in bed hurting, she decided that he might not be faking it after all, and she took him to the doctor.

As they sat in the waiting room, Mama warned him, "Alan, you don't have to tell the doctor that Bill hurt your foot."

When the doctor asked, "Good evening young man. What happened to your foot?" Alan quickly responded, "Somebody pushed me down the steps, but Mother told me not to tell who did it!"

The doctor later discovered two broken bones in Alan's foot.

So goes one of our most-repeated family stories, told by the mom who became my mother when I married her son. My second mother was and is a masterful storyteller.

"I've been praying for you ever since Bill was a baby."

This opening story line began my love relationship with the woman who became "Mama" to me. From the moment I met her, I experienced such acceptance that I wanted to be my best in her presence. Mama is the transparent vessel of Jesus Christ in the way she tells her stories, and in the way she loves people through them.

How does she do this? I've asked myself that question a thousand times. And I've yet to find a complete answer. But I know parts of it. Mama is neither braggish, nor wormish. She is simply happy being Beverly. Because she believes in her own worth as well as the worth of every person she encounters, she's able to do "what God's will is—His good, pleasing, and perfect will" (Romans 12:2). She's a master at story-living and story-telling. And in the living and telling of her life, she shows the Master, God himself. Each day is a new episode for her, to be lived with great eagerness for whatever is on the next page. And Mama seems to believe that each story is best when shared with others.

"We have a story to tell you!" she says nearly every time we see her. She once told us about entering a house with what she called "very unusual inhabitants." She took fifteen delicious minutes to hold us in suspense, then with a twinkle in her eye, she told of her encounter with fleas! They jumped on her legs, got in her clothing and made her itch for days. Instead of grumbling about deplorable conditions, Mama chose to make them into a hilarious story.

My mama shows this same interest in detail whether the experience is easy or painful. When our young daughters encountered sickness and disability, she agonized with us through those long nights and night-marish days. She'd listen with interest to every detail of what I'd tell her, and then knew just what to say or do to genuinely help. From my mama I've learned the delight of sharing life, of hearing and resonating with every aspect of a loved one's story.

My mama uses her stories to grow roots of joy and connectedness.

"Tell us a little-Bill-Dockrey story Grandmamma!" my children ask her, anxious to hear another story about their daddy as a little boy. She tells equally interesting stories about them as little girls: "Do you remember when Sarah had just learned to walk and kept tumbling down the hill during the Easter egg hunt? Undaunted, she would stand right back up and try again. She couldn't figure why the slanted yard didn't work like the floors she'd been practicing on. But she found a way to walk on that non-flat surface. Sarah, you still have that same adventuresome spirit—determined not to miss even a second of life.

"And do you remember when Emily was a tiny baby and we met halfway between our houses to visit? It started to rain just as we unbuckled her car seat. We scooped baby Emily up, ran into the hotel room, and closed the door in her parent's faces! Emily, your daddy still gives us a hard time about that, saying he knew then who the really important one was. And he was right; you were always irreplaceably valuable to us, Emily."

My mama's stories make every listener feel deeply cherished, never humiliated or criticized. Her stories are an act of worship, a declaration that each person matters and that each event in life is important.

Perhaps more importantly, my mama lives her stories. Whether it's a trip to the grocery store or to the Grand Canyon, she approaches it with a sense of fun. Whether it's a story about today or an event that happened to one of her ancestors, Mama wants to understand every exploit. She looks to the past and the future with eagerness to learn, and then lives, firmly in the present, those lessons learned.

In the nearly twenty years I've known and loved Mama, she has taught me to delight in the story of my life. As one who tends to criticize and complain, I am learning from her that whining and worrying only steal the fun.

A classic example came last April when my family and I went to a state park for the day. Bill and I had combed the grocery aisles for fun picnic foods, and I'd planned just how to organize them in the cooler so the foods wouldn't get soaked by the iced drinks. I packed according to plan. At lunch we opened the cooler only to discover I had totally forgotten to put the ice in! The day became one joke after another about forgetting ice for the ice chest.

As I telephoned my mother-in-law to tell her the ice chest story, I realized that she was the one who had instilled this make-an-adventure attitude in me. The chapters of Mama's life continue to be written through her children and grandchildren. I pray that the sequel to my life would be just as purely written in my descendants. I pray that each word I write with my voice and my actions will be one my family and friends will delight in reading over and over again.

Karen Dockrey with a home base of Hendersonville, Tennessee, is a busy writer, mother, and youth worker. The recent publication of two books, *Growing a Family Where People Really Like Each Other* by Bethany House Publishers, and *Tuned Up Parenting* by Victor Books, brings her total number of books to twenty-five. When she is not writing, she spends time with her daughters, and volunteers with youth in her church. Karen's mother-in-law, Beverly Dockrey, lives in Madisonville, Kentucky.

CHAPTER SIX

BALLOONS FOR MOTHER
by Marlene LeFevere

I didn't buy my mother a balloon, and I've been sorry ever since. The lions were in the ring and the clowns were falling all over themselves. Popcorn, noise, roars: she and I loved the circus. All we two fully grown women needed to make our day perfect was a helium-filled balloon.

But three dollars? We both remembered my growing up years when our Friday nights were spent walking and talking through the downtown stores—with fifty cents between us. I just couldn't bring myself to splurge by paying three dollars for a balloon for my mother.

Too bad! Balloons are a perfect metaphor for the atmosphere mother created for my brother and me as we were growing up. She filled our lives with creative balloons. They weren't the circus ones that fly away or bust. They were, instead, the many experiences that helped mold and challenge us both.

If we were at the circus today, I would buy the biggest balloon I could find and present it to Mother. "Thanks for all the ideas, hours and excitement," I'd say. "Thanks for the balloons with which you filled my childhood."

We had the only basement in town with a life-sized, motorized whale in it. I was with Mother the day she got it. She went into the supermarket and asked the manager what he was going to do with the big fish opening and shutting its mouth over the tuna display.

"Don't toss it," Mother begged. "It would make a great visual aid for the story of Jonah." Mother was always looking for better ways to communicate with children—my brother Jim and me, all the neighborhood kids and the thousands of children who have been part of her Bible classes.

I don't think my mother ever thought, "How can I force my kids to use all the creativity God gave them?" She just loved doing fun things with us and watching in wonder to see which one of us would come up with something unexpected.

"I'm so proud of you," she would tell my brother after he built one of his amazing creations in our basement. "No one else in this family is the least bit mechanical." He would proudly hold her verbal balloon, and the next time my father announced that something couldn't be fixed, Jim would fix it.

From my mother I learned that money has nothing much to do with creativity. My mother was always looking for what was different, unusual, fun.

I remember one evening Mother stuck her head in the door and whispered, "Marlene, is your father home yet?" No, he wasn't.

"Thank goodness!" she said. "I've just spent a dollar on a piece of fuzzy paper." Mother's food budget was very small, and a dollar would be missed, but she was obviously too excited about the paper to care. She unrolled it, and sure enough, it was fuzzy and red. Today, felt paper is common, but this was the first time any of us had seen it. "Look at this," she said as she rubbed her finger across the paper. "It makes a mark. But not to worry." She rubbed the paper the opposite direction and the mark disappeared. Then she said the most creative line a parent can use. "Now what can we do with it?"

I'd never remember what we could have eaten with that dollar, but I'll never forget what we did with the fuzzy paper. We cut it out and used it to make two beautiful valentine bows to take to school, where our teachers and friends could share in mother's wonderful find.

Mother never passed up a missionary or other special Christians who might enlarge her children's lives.

I spent many a childhood night sleeping on the living room sofa so a missionary could have my bed. Some of those people treated me, a young girl, like a "real" person, sharing their aspirations, successes and hardships. Because of my mother's hospitality, I grew up knowing that the world God had given was bigger than the farm I grew up on— much, much bigger.

My mother was always watching for special moments that might never come again. She would always drop whatever she was doing to enjoy those moments with us.

One day, my younger brother Jim sat at the window and watched the rain pound. With his finger he traced the path of drops over the glass. Mom was writing letters in the same room, but it was as if she said to herself, "I have never seen Jim doing that before. Maybe he'll never be as interested in raindrops again." She put down the letter and moved over to the window. For a long time, mother and son sat together and made map-paths following the drops flow. A super highway was over to the left, a windy path through the center must be the race track, and over there....

My mother taught me that work may never be really fun, but it can be creative. We would play word games while we worked. She would say a word and I would have to come up with another word that began with the same letter with which the word ended. Or for even more fun, we would sing our conversations! As I got older we would sing in rhyming couplets. Dusting, making beds and sweeping the floor were never things I looked forward to, but I never dreaded them either.

As kids, when my brother or I made a mess of things in the house, Mother seemed to know our hearts were in the right place, so she made the messes beautiful. For example, a missionary who stayed in our home shared how the earthquakes in Greece had been devastating. He told how children in the orphanages that he ran would be cold that winter unless Christians helped. As an almost-eight-year-old, I responded. One afternoon when my mother was running an errand, I took my wagon to the neighboring farms, explained the plight of the orphans and asked for clothes and blankets. I brought each load home and dumped it in the middle of the living room. When my mother arrived and saw the mess that I'd made of her home, she was delighted. "If we use the car," she said, "we can get even more." By the end of our collection, our family had collected more than 2000 pounds of clothing for those orphanages in Greece.

Several years after my mother died, I shared this story as part of a speech I was giving. A woman came up afterwards and said, "I thank God that your mother loved serving Jesus more than a clean house. I was one of those orphans."

On the first morning of my first trip home after starting college, I woke up around 5 a.m. to the smell of pork chops. Minutes later here came Mom into my bedroom with three perfectly broiled pork chops. "I knew they were your favorite and I didn't want you to ever forget your first breakfast home." Mother was always sending up balloons of creativity.

When she died, she left me a legacy of greater value than money, one that demands of me, "Be as creative as God meant for you to be."

Marlene LeFevere is Manager of Ministry Relations for David C. Cook Church Ministries. She has authored more than ten books, among them *Learning Styles: Reaching Everyone God Gave You to Teach* (Cook) and *Creative Teaching Methods* (Cook). Marlene has served as adjunct faculty at many colleges and universities including Princeton Seminary, Talbot Theological Seminary and Denver Seminary. Each year, Marlene speaks to more than 10,000 Christian education volunteers across the United States and around the world. Her mother, Naomi Ruth LeFevere, was a Child Evangelism and Sunday school teacher who was as inventive and fresh then in her teaching approach as her daughter is now.

CHAPTER SEVEN

WHAT PICKING APPLES TAUGHT ME ABOUT MY MOTHER
by Karen Burton Mains

Picking apples early one fall morning brought me face-to-face with memories of my mother.

"Watch down below!" my son-in-law shouted before shaking the apple tree. A ladder boosted him up into the center of the primary branches. "Out of the way!" he cried again, a second before a rain of fruit began to pummel the ground, apples hailing down upon the soft earth and grass.

Caitlyn, my three-year-old granddaughter, laughed; we adults—my pregnant daughter, my son-in-law, and myself—while babysitting that morning for my son and his wife, felt the wonder of apple picking again. Gnarled and worm-holed but nevertheless tasty, the fruit was collected into three galvanized tubs, toted into the bathroom, and washed by Caitlyn and her Uncle Doug in the bath. Racing a September rainstorm all morning, we were eager to make it to the Elburn cider press before afternoon.

The cider press was a two-story affair, housed in an old white-washed shed, part of the working tradition of a three-generation family. Just as the clouds released their thunder, we pulled into the driveway, tugged the tubs of apples into the shelter, then waited for the farmer and his father to arrive. During the short interlude, I noticed their apples sitting in baskets from their orchard—all round and shining, perfect in matching, rosy symmetry. In preparation for our apples, the wife began emptying the vats of standing cider. Her five-year-old daughter, the model of tidy efficiency, appeared from what seemed like nowhere and began carrying two plastic jugs at a time to the refrigerator. While waiting, I bought some of their cider and a jar of homemade jam.

"Your trees need pruning," said the farmer as he started the antique apparatus, dumping our misshapen fruit onto the conveyer belt. "We had them pruned last spring," Doug objected, but the comparison between our deformed orphans and the glowing, perfect mounds of fruit in the nearby baskets was all too obvious. "Need to have them pruned more," the expert replied. "I can tell by their shapes."

By this time the tumbling apples were turning into mash, hidden blades chopping stems and seeds and skin and flesh. The grandfather arrived and hurried to help move the large weights into place. "This hasn't been a good apple year," said the farmer as more apples rode topside to be converted into pulp. "In fact, yours are the first we've pressed besides our own."

Caitlyn's eyes took it all in. The bouncing apples. The busy little girl toting bottles, opening and closing the refrigerator door. The chopped mash. The grandfather. "Oh, look Caitlyn," said Melissa to her little niece. "Watch down there. Watch and see the cider coming from our apples." We crouched and located the tube where the juices were starting to flow.

"See. Those are the weights that press the mash and all the juices come running out."

The two men lifted the weights into place, then cranked the handle that lowered the press. Lovely golden nectar began to flow, eventually filling seven gallon jugs. Pulling myself away from all this drama, I hastened through the rain to meet a friend for lunch. But I was told that Caitlyn, when given a small sample cup of cider, refused to share it. "No" she said to Melissa. "This is mine. This is mine." Not selfishness here; justifiable reward. After all, like the little red hen, she had picked the apples, she had washed them, she had toted them to the press. This was the fair fruit of her efforts.

With windshield wipers beating rhythm, I thought of the joys of grandparenting, how it is we are granted a chance to live again the moments of wonder and awe and delight; how little ones lead us back, give us once more the opportunity to savor, to pause and sip, to laugh and be riotous, to snuggle and be intimate, to be wise about the potential richness of all moments.

And I noted how much my daughter's conversation, as we waited in that little shed, with all the apples bumping and the rain pouring outside, was about the ways of her grandmother, my mother ("Dobie" to her grandchildren). "I remember when Dobie and Bompa took us to the State Fair. Dobie always had those windmill cookies with chopped walnuts in the cookie jar. And Dreamcicles in the freezer. Whenever we were at her house, we could just help ourselves."

Mother lives in her grandchildren's memories (as I am determined I will weave my life into the memories of my grandchildren). There are many gifts my mother gave to me, but the one which I'm only beginning to realize is this: my mother taught me how to be a good grandmother.

Obviously, this is an art, lore best passed from generation to generation. And it seems to me that good grandmothering consists of many things. It is intentionally creating happy memories for all the decades that follow; it is a matter of providing joyful learning experiences; it is a spiritual calling to pass on the values that conserve the Christian ethos. But most of all, as millions of grandparents testify, it is a way of delight.

My mother saw her grandchildren weekly. I have drastically reduced my travel schedule and writing obligations in order to have enough life to share abundantly with my adult children and with their children. I want the next generations to feel as at home in my house as they do in their own homes. Caitlyn knows where the silverware drawer is, where her toys are stored, which flowers in the cutting gardens she is allowed to pick, and where her sleepy-time doll and blanket are. (I must remember, however, to stock up on the Dreamcicles.)

My mother knew that she was the connective tissue of history. Knowledge of what has been and of how to do would be lost if she hadn't bestowed it. And I hear myself passing on her wisdom as she passed it onto me.

Children's play has always been sacred to me. Here, in how a child focuses, in where his or her interests are attached, are the clues to what the future can be. So we test in this serious activity called play. Caitlyn, even as a little girl, can stick with the tasks; at two years old she helped me plant a hundred tulip bulbs; this spring she spent an hour doggedly dragging pruned branches to the brush pile, this fall she gathered the apples. Though shy, she is not afraid. "I want to do that,"she has said—about riding the train, going motorcycling, ice skating, etc. When I took her pony riding, to my horror the pony bolted, throwing my granddaughter to the ground. "Ponies do this sometimes," I explained, remembering my own mother's momilies. "This time I'll hold on tighter—to you and to the horsie."

After wiping tears and giving comfort, she remounted and we rode for another half an hour until I was sure her uncertainties had been put to ease. Knowing, however, the trickiness of the ponies is an important lesson. "Ponies can do this," I said to my fearless three-year-old. "We don't have to be afraid, but we do need to be careful."

Like my mother before me, I am the connective tissue now between time present and time past. Like my mother before me, I interpret to Caitlyn's parents; "You know this really is a remarkable characteristic. This child is not afraid of new experiences. She is not timid to try out life. Many children would not be able to get back up on the pony."

One of the major callings these days—during these decades of my fifties, sixties, seventies and, if God grants the time, eighties—is to help form the continual becoming of my adult children and that of my grandchildren—of Caitlyn and Landis, of baby Nathaniel, of the embryo even now stretching in my daughter's womb, and of all those who will be the sons and daughters of my other children. These are not the days primarily for self discovery (though that really never ceases), these are not the years when I want to make a name for myself or give away my energy to strangers. No, like my mother before me, who had a grandchild or several under her wing, these are the times to concentrate on forming the generations behind me.

This is how juice is made from apples; there must be pressure to create cider....

This is how we get back up when we have fallen....

This is who God is and how he works in our lives....

"Things that we have heard and know, that our fathers (and mothers) have told us. We will not hide them from our children, but tell to the coming generation the glorious deeds of the Lord, and his might...which he commanded to our fathers (and mothers) to teach to their children; that the next generation might know them, the children yet unborn, and arise and tell them to their children, so that they should set their hope in God..." Psalm 78:3–6.

This is my work, my calling, for the decades ahead. And this I learned from my mother, Wilma Wicklund Burton. She taught (and teaches me still) how to be a good grandmother.

Karen Burton Mains is an author, with more than twelve books to her credit, and an articulate communicator who is actively involved in radio and television broadcasting. She is the author of the best selling *Open Heart, Open Home,* as well as hostess of *The Chapel of the Air,* an internationally syndicated daily radio program. Karen and her husband David have raised four children and currently live in the Chicago area. Karen's mother, Wilma Wicklund Burton, spent her adult life as a devoted and faithful worker with parachurch organizations. She and her husband, Wilfred, a music professor at Moody Bible Institute for thirty-three years, raised three children, all of whom are involved in full-time Christian service. In addition, Mrs. Burton was a prize-winning poet and the editor of a national literary magazine, and she authored three books during the several years before she died in 1982. She was awarded an honorary doctorate for her writing, and her grandchildren still remark about how she modeled unusual joy in living.

CHAPTER EIGHT

THE JOYFUL POET
by Dee Brestin

How will I remember Mother?

Will it be as Gretel in the operetta of *Hansel and Gretel?* I was one of thousands of school children captivated by the sight of her slim, graceful form swirling about the stage in a red dirndl skirt and vest, black braids framing her exquisite face as she sang in her lovely soprano voice. "That is my mother," I said proudly to my friends.

Or will it be as Winnie-the-Pooh stuck in Rabbit's hole and moaning, "Oh, what is a bear who loves honey so to do?" Our five-year-old son J. R. said, "That is my Grandma!"

Perhaps it will be as the Dowager Empress in Escondido's magnificent production of *Anastasia.* Mother, then nearly seventy, made the audience weep—and ponder man's inhumanity to man.

May I never forget her laughter, or her joy in life. When she and Dad toured a California winery, he went to the rest room and returned to find Mother in the vat, arm-in-arm with twenty others, circling, singing, and stomping grapes. None of her children or twelve grandchildren were surprised by this. As I write this, she and Dad are preparing to fly to Paris to celebrate their sixtieth anniversary, and Mother's letters are filled with the joy of anticipation. My dad often quotes, "A merry heart doeth good like medicine" (Proverbs 17:22a) in regard to Mother's mother and to Mother. Oh Lord, may my children remember me in that way, too.

I will always associate Mother with the sound of her singing, always singing. Lullabies, show tunes, hymns, and operas. We never traveled in the car, whether it was a mile to the Piggly Wiggly or three thousand miles to Mexico, without singing. We sang *May the Good Lord Bless and Keep You, Oh What a Beautiful Morning, Over the River and through the Woods* and countless others.

We were a church-going family and both of my parents had high moral values, but our church was not a strong Bible-preaching church. In fact, I didn't understand the central message of the Bible or put my trust in Christ until I was in my twenties. I was familiar with many scriptures because I had heard them sung by Mother. In church and at home I often heard Mother sing *The Lord is My Light and My Salvation.* Recently Mother said these comforting words to me: "When life was cruel, I would sing that song—and believe it."

As children we knew the Christmas carols—and sang all the verses. I believe that the words to those songs helped to prepare and soften my heart when I was presented with the gospel as a young wife and mother. In October of 1966, I pondered whether or not to put my trust in Christ. I had been presented with the claims of Christ: that he claimed to be God, to have died for my sins—and to have risen again! Therefore he wanted me to surrender my life to him. If I rejected him, I would face God's wrath without a Savior. Was it true? Or was it a fairy tale?

During the next month I read the entire New Testament. I cried out to God, and pleaded with him (if he existed!) to show me the truth. During that month, as I was washing dishes, or walking, or nursing my baby—the lyrics Mother sang kept floating in my mind:

"I wonder as I wander, out under the sky, how Jesus the Savior did come for to die, for poor, orn'ry people like you and like I...."

"Fall on your knees. Oh hear the angel voices! O night divine, O night when Christ was born!"

"The Lord is my light, and my salvation, whom then shall I fear...?"

God in his mercy helped me to see that I was a sinner, that I should fall on my knees in repentance—and that he would be my light and my salvation. As I surrendered to him, his mercy poured out on me, not only assuring me of salvation, but opening my eyes to a whole world I had not even known existed.

Mother not only surrounded us with music but with art as well. Prints from Renoir, Van Gogh, and many of the masters filled our home. She herself was gifted artistically—and her paintings surround me still: of lions that she and Dad saw on their safari to Africa, of sails bellied out on Green Bay, and of Queen Anne's Lace and forget-me-nots spreading abundantly across the meadows of Wisconsin. She saw what so many, in the busyness of life, missed. And she taught us to see, too.

Mother passed on to me an appreciation for the artistic. Because of her influence I realize the importance of drawing upon the best in drama, music, literature, and art in order to express in my writing and speaking the truths God has impressed upon my heart.

Mother had a dream as a young woman that she began to see fulfilled two years before I was born. She wanted to begin a children's theater in our city and present the best, and only the best, in children's plays and musicals. Together with Mother, a core of women began with the operetta of *Hansel and Gretel.* It was so successful that it was repeated years later, when I was a second-grader. The original score of this operetta has a deeply spiritual message, as I am convinced the best in art always does.

I can still remember, though it has been more than forty years, the sight of Hansel and Gretel praying beneath the towering trees of the forest while singing *The Children's Prayer* and *God Our Father* and pleading for help to overcome the cruel forces of evil in their young lives. When they were re-united with their father and danced for joy, we in the audience rejoiced as well. And those who knew Christ may have perceived the spiritual message—that God cares for children and listens to their prayers.

When Mother cast *Heidi* completely with children, we learned, through working on that beautiful story, the power of love to transform lives. Thank you, Mother, for teaching me that truth at such a tender age—in a way I could not forget.

As a teenager, Mother worked with me for hours as I learned my lines for plays, declamations, or sometimes just a simple presentation to the family. As the words from those gifted writers became a part of me, they changed me. I still remember lines from *The Diary of Anne Frank*, *The Merchant of Venice* and *Our Town*. I played the part of Emily in *Our Town*. There is a particularly poignant scene where young Emily, who has died and gone to Heaven, looks back on earth. She asks, "Does anyone ever realize life while they are living it? Hot baths, and waking up, and Mama, and Papa..." The reply is, "The poets and the saints—they do, some."

With Mother as my model, my husband and I have raised our five children to act out the stories of Scripture, to take Proverbs such as "A soft answer turns away wrath" and turn them into a simple skit. One of the most effective Sunday school classes my husband and I ever led was a class in which ten families, among other things, sang praise choruses together and acted out two minute "Proverb Skits" for each other. Today our five nearly grown children love the Lord, know the Scriptures, and either are or will be the kind of parents who avoid dull family devotions!

My prayer for myself echoes the lines from *Our Town* which I learned with my mother so long ago: Oh Lord, may I realize this life now, while I am living it. Thank you for giving me Mother, and may I pass on to the next generation what I learned from her—an appreciation for the beauty in your world, and the importance of telling the message as vividly and as clearly as possible.

Dee Brestin is a national retreat speaker and author of the best-selling book, *The Friendships of Women*, as well as, *We Are Sisters*, and her own line of Bible study guides for women. Dee has five children and two grandchildren, and she makes her home in Kearney, Nebraska. Her mother, Marianne Kirkland Brown, just celebrated her sixtieth wedding anniversary and continues to live life to its fullest. Mrs. Brown sings, paints, and writes faithfully to her daughters. She has even written a book for her grandchildren and great grandchildren.

CHAPTER NINE

FOUND OUT!
by Lori Wick

*D*id you have fun at Patty's?" my mom asked me as soon as I came in the door.

"Yes. We rode horses!" I lied enthusiastically, my face alive with my fantasy. (What Patty and I had actually done was stand at the fence and *look* at the neighbor's horses. We didn't even touch them.)

"You did?" My mother's face was skeptical.

"Yes." I continued the fantasy. "We rode for miles and miles."

"Lori." This time, my mother's tone was unbelieving. "The area around Patty's house is all fenced off. How could you have ridden for miles?"

I had to think fast. "The horses just jumped. They did, Mom, they really did. When the horses came to the fences they just jumped over 'em."

"Are you telling me the truth, Lori?"

It was a question I'd heard many times over the years. But this time I didn't come around with the truth. Later that evening, my lie was found out when we went to visit our pastor, who also happened to have horses. I was awestruck to be so close to these huge animals that I loved. When the pastor realized my fascination, he boosted me into the saddle. The horse never moved, not one step was taken, but I was frozen with fear. I can still see my mother's face and I can hear her say, "This is the girl who rode a horse that jumped fences this afternoon."

I have often wondered how my mother so skillfully managed to deal with the times I told her untruths. She would always confront me when she suspected I was adding to the truth or out-and-out lying. And I was punished for my sin.

At the same time my mother never squelched the creativity that poured out of me in my wild childish fantasies. My imagination was always at work. My dolls and pets talked to me, and I often had monsters in the closet that I was certain would stay there if Mom would only leave the light on until I fell asleep. I was never out of stories or high drama and Mom was never out of smiles, forgiveness, and loving arms to hold me even when I had trouble distinguishing truth from untruth.

Although my mother was very excited when I began to write fiction, I don't think she was too surprised. I had long since given up my ways of fantasizing real-life adventures, but as someone once said, "As a child you're a liar, as an adult you're a fiction writer." That isn't my mother's quote, but it could be. Long before she knew I would be a writer, she saw up close and personal what kind of person it would take to create such vivid and varied stories. But as a child, she never allowed me to compromise on the truth.

My mother is very artistic. She draws beautifully. I used to gaze in awe at the drawings she saved from high school, and whenever the *TV Guide* had an ad for an art school, my mother would copy those little sample pictures to perfection. My mother also used her creativity to create a haven of warmth and caring for my father, my brother and me. She made home a special place. Her budget was not huge, yet the house was decorated tastefully and she allowed my brother and me to express ourselves in our own bedrooms. She always seemed to understand the importance of creativity.

But the thing that sticks out in my mind the most about my mother are the worn pages in her Bible. I remember getting a new Bible when I was in junior high school and desperately wanting the pages to be as soft and easy to turn as my mother's were. I knew well how they'd gotten that way. My mother was my earliest example of one who believed that time spent with God was the most precious time of all. I've been a published author for just six years now, but in that time, and in the years before, I've learned from my mother that nothing is at peak performance without taking time alone with God.

My mother taught me truthfulness. She allowed for my creativity, but more importantly she taught me that I simply cannot be the woman God wants me to be unless I meet and talk with him every single day.

Lori Wick is a well-loved Christian fiction writer whose latest books include *Sophie's Heart, Where the Wild Rose Blooms* and *Whispers of Moonlight.* Even though Lori lives in Mazomanie, Wisconsin, and her mother, Pearl Hayes, lives in Santa Rosa, California, they keep in close touch. When they do get together, they can often be found curled up on the couch with a bag of popcorn watching old movies and musicals.

CHAPTER TEN

DR. DENTON'S PAJAMAS NEVER FELT SO GOOD
by Ruth Flesvig Gibson

I felt hot and confined in my Dr. Denton pajamas with the drop-seat and closed-in feet. So, I got out of bed and went downstairs into the bright living room to find Dad reading and Mom mending. I was three years old and it felt secure to see my parents sitting there together.

I told Mom I wanted to wiggle my toes to cool my hot feet. I boldly asked her to please cut the feet off my Dr. Denton pajamas. Mom took the scissors from the sewing basket and carefully cut the feet out of my pajamas right there as I wore them. I looked down at the freshly cut, slightly ragged cuffs and dug my liberated little toes into the deep, rose-colored carpet. I was amazed that my mother had granted my request so readily. I know now that she probably weighed the cost of Dr. Dentons and evaluated the amount of wear I had left in them before she took out her scissors. But, by granting my simple request, my mother gave me the assurance that adults, and God Himself, can reasonably consider my needs and wishes. It is an assurance that has never left me.

Mother's responses taught me about God's care. They also taught me about God's forgiveness. I remember one time when I was about six years old and our family visited some friends in New York City. The adults tucked me and my brother and sister into bed and went to talk in the living room. Soon, the three of us kids crawled out from under our covers and began jumping from one bed to the other, as if on trampolines.

My mother soon appeared in the doorway, a look of disappointment on her face. She said nothing, but simply sat down in a chair in the corner, her head in her hands. No lecture. No scolding. Not a word. But, oh, the impact of that eloquent maternal silence! We children promptly slipped back under our covers without a sound and soon fell asleep.

Next morning, nothing was said about our mischief of the night before. To this day, Mother has never mentioned the incident. But I can tell you, I've never jumped on a bed since! My mom's wise nonverbal discipline, and her restraint of any lingering recriminations over the bed-jumping caper, later helped me understand the meaning of Psalm 103:12—"As far as the east is from the west, so far has he removed our transgressions from us."

From Mom, I learned the meaning of hard work.

After teaching for many years in the Chicago Public Schools on a two-year teaching certificate, Mom went back to college and got her bachelor's degree in education. She did this during my sophomore year in college. I came home to watch her get her diploma in cap and gown. What an inspiration! She glowed as she came down the aisle, pleased with her honor as the first one in her family to earn a college degree. From Mom's experience came a focused piece of advice for facing tasks I'd rather avoid—"Just do it!" Believe me, I did! Mom always advised, "Get a teaching certificate." I did that, too!

Working as hard as she did at home and school, Mom gave me an example of partnership with Dad. Dad had his own business but often said he was able to succeed because Mom pulled with him in contributing to the family income. The memory of their fifty-two years of pulling together continues to invigorate my own marriage.

Now I find myself well into the sandwich years, having to function as parent toward my own adult children and toward my mother, who is ninety. Today I went to a party at the retirement center where she lives. Because of her declining capabilities, she now resides in the medical wing with nursing care. Julia, the activities director at this facility, makes the place as much fun as a Caribbean cruise. In fact, I refer to her as the Cruise Director. On party days like today, I generally meet my mother in "Medical." Then I take her in a wheel chair to the other side of the complex, where the healthier, more independent people live. Today, as I came into Medical to get Mom, I found her with her friends, listening to a man in a Hawaiian shirt play the guitar. She was having such fun I decided not to disturb her good time.

I'll just go down the corridor to the main building where the celebration is being held for the volunteers, I thought to myself, remembering the purpose of the day's planned party. When I got to the other side of the building, I saw the festive tables with hors d'oeuvres. But only three people had gathered so far. I chatted with them for a minute or two, but I soon realized that most of the people I knew were still in the other wing, having fun with the man in the Hawaiian shirt. Then in a flash it hit me: *my mother is on the other side.*

As I pensively walked back down the corridor, I savored the fresh awareness that, for my mother and all of us who belong to Christ, the party is on the other side. The momentary struggles and joys of her earthly life will fade in the brilliance of that party prepared for her on the other side.

As I experience the twilight of my mother's life, I think often of the legacy she will leave behind. She taught me well that people are available to listen to me and respond to my needs and that you can sometimes make an impact most eloquently without words. Through her, I have learned in hard times to "just do it." And as I watch her enjoying her twilight years, I have great peace and optimism about my own aging and about being able to see the good in every season of life.

Ruth Flesvig Gibson makes her home in Wheaton, Illinois, where she and her husband direct Wheaton Counseling Associates, Ltd. Ruth also hosts a local cable TV talk show, runs a program at her church for mothers of preschoolers, and writes. Her most recent book is *The Sandwich Years* by Baker Book House. Ruth's mother, Ruth Erickson Flesvig currently lives in the Windsor Park Manor in Carol Stream, Illinois. Mrs. Flesvig was a school teacher in Chicago's public schools for many years. One of the special things that Ruth and her mother do each Christmas Eve is to prepare a Swedish Smorgasbord for the family.

CHAPTER ELEVEN

"OH GOD, MAKE ME A GOOD MOTHER"
by Jill Briscoe

I suppose one of the worst journeys of my life was the one I took from Capenwray, my home in northern England, down to Liverpool where my mother lived. I was on my way to tell her that we were moving to America. Mother had been recently widowed; my sister, Shirley, and I and our families were all she had left. And now, I'd come with the news that Stuart and I were leaving—taking her three grandchildren across the Atlantic to a new home.

I could see the look of utter dismay on her face. The first thing she said was, "How could you? How could you leave me?"

And then, before she even caught her breath, she went on to say, "Oh, but how selfish could I be? Of course you must go. You must be with Stuart. Please forgive me."

And from that time on she was perfectly willing to have us go. In fact, she sent us off with her blessing, reassuring us that she only wanted the best for us.

Mother never came to see us in America. She was afraid of closed spaces so she could never fly. In the eleven years from the time we left England until her death, we only saw her a few times. But she never complained about the fact that we did not have the money to go running back and forth across the Atlantic. We never heard a word about how awful it was that we had taken her grandchildren from her. Mother was so committed to what was best for her children that it overshadowed any thought or concern she had for her own well-being.

Perhaps she had learned that type of intense commitment to her children, no matter the cost to her, because she had mothered us through a very trying wartime situation in England.

My most poignant memory of my mother is the time during the Blitz. My father was in the Air Force so he was gone. From 5 P.M. to 5 A.M., my mother, my sister and I slept in the air raid shelters.

Then one night, a bomb damaged a part of our house.

I will never forget the night after the bomb fell. I'd been home from school because I was sick. My sister and I were playing cards. The TV was on. Suddenly, my mother said, "Be quiet. Prime Minister Churchill is going to speak."

And sure enough, there was the Prime Minister saying, "We will fight on the seas and oceans...we shall fight in the fields, and in the streets, we shall fight in the hills; we shall never surrender..." And then he went on to issue the command that all people living on the coastline of England (and that included us) should pack as quickly as possible. If the church bells rang, that would be the signal the invasion had begun and we should be prepared to run.

I was terrified.

"Where will we go?" I asked my mother.

"We will go and God will take care of us," my mother answered.

My father, home on leave, whisked us away up to the Lake District. We had no place to live but my father was able to find a houseboat for us. Mother hated the water. She couldn't swim. But she moved us onto that boat, put us into a dinghy every morning so we could go to school, and sat it out on that boat until we could get other temporary accommodations.

How did she do it?

She did it scared. Every night she put the rope of the dinghy through the porthole and tied it around her wrist in case we needed to get off the boat quickly! She did everything she could to keep us safe, to keep us alive. I knew my mother would fight for us, that she would die for us if she needed to. My mother modeled guts, stick-ability, how to tough it out in the hard times. Through her I learned I can do it scared, too. And most of the time, even today, I run scared. But I do whatever I have to do anyway, even if I am scared. That is my mother in me.

My mother modeled trust. I grew up knowing she was trusting God. And years later, when I came to faith as a college student at a teachers' college in Cambridge, it was easy for me to come. I understood trust because I had a mother who lived trust before us every day of her life.

Another quality of life I profited from was my mother's sense of openness and honesty. She could never bear to harbor anything and had to "have it out" as soon as possible. She always had to tell us what was on her mind and clear the air. I'm sure it was this healthy training that helped me later to keep things right in my relationship with God and thus keep the lines open to heaven.

I also saw, from my mother's example, how to manage without a husband for long stretches of time. During the war, because my father was in the Air Force, we were separated from him for the best part of five years. But I never heard Mother complain about his being gone. She just did what she had to do, and that was to see to it that my sister and I were taken care of.

And when I married Stuart and he became an evangelist, traveling around the world preaching, it was easier (though not always *that* easy) for me to have him gone for long periods of time because I'd seen my mother's strength and courage when my father was gone.

My mother was intense about her mothering, committed to us but not controlling or overly protective of us. She prayed diligently for us. She also prayed for herself. After I was grown and had left home, my mother told me she prayed this prayer every day of her life: "Oh God, make me a good mother."

I thought about my mother's prayer the day we brought our first-born, David, home from the hospital. Stuart and I had decided I would go home to be with my mother for a while so she could help us. I'll never forget standing there in my old pink and white room, my tiny son in my arms and feeling totally awed by my new responsibility as a mother. Then suddenly, I remembered the prayer my mother had prayed. I knelt by my bed and I prayed the same prayer, "Oh God, make me a good mother." And then I added, "like Peggy." (From our early childhood days my mother had asked us to call her Peggy because she was determined to be our friend as well as our mother.)

I have prayed that prayer many times since that day so long ago. And every time, I think of my mother, of her simple trust and of how thoroughly God has answered her prayer. She was indeed a good mother—even more, a wonderful one. And I am a better person today because of it.

Jill Briscoe is the author of more than forty books, the most recent being *It Had to be a Monday*, published by Tyndale House Publishers. Besides her active speaking ministry, she finds time for women's ministry in the Elmbrook Church, near Milwaukie, Wisconsin, where her husband Stuart is the pastor. Jill is the mother of three adult children and nine grandchildren. Her mother, Peggy Ryder, was of Scottish origin but lived in England for many years. Mrs. Ryder married young and brought up two daughters—Jill and her sister, Shirley. She died in England at the age of seventy-two.

Chapter Twelve

A NEW WAY TO SPELL MOM
by Judy Briscoe Golz

Many years ago, my mom wrote a poem to me thanking me for being her friend. Yet it is her friendship that has helped me become the woman I am today. I spell Mom this way: F-R-I-E-N-D.

"F" is for faithful. I have seen my mother's faithfulness to God in her walk with Him and in how she serves others. Mom and I teach a seminar together on the book of Ruth. One of the things we try to do is describe the different types of love demonstrated in the Bible. One definition of *agapé*, or God's love, is to be primarily concerned with another's well-being regardless of the cost to yourself. My mother has always demonstrated this type of love to me. In our family, we tease Mom because she is the defender of the family—always looking out for everyone else's well-being, making sure we're all happy and content, putting herself last, never first. She has given me a wonderful example of how to demonstrate God's love to those around me.

Mom's devotion to God and her wholehearted determination to spend her life serving Him has challenged me in my Christian walk. I've always marveled at how reading the Bible and praying is so integrated into her life that it just seems to happen each day. I have struggled with trying to find the "right" time to have a quiet time. What Mom has taught me is that there probably isn't just one right time. I need to grab the moment each day.

She told me that when my brothers and I were small, she couldn't find time to read her Bible so she decided just to leave it open on the kitchen counter. As she went about her busy day, whenever she passed the counter, she'd read another verse and then think about it. I've used

Mom's idea—leaving my Bible open, reading a few paragraphs of a Christian book or magazine article, listening to a sermon. I'm still working on this issue, but Mom's faithful example helps me keep trying.

"R" is for relational. My mom is one of my best friends. Even during the years when I was a teenager and more interested in spending time with my friends than with my mother, she tried to find things that she knew I would like doing so that we could spend time together. One of those things was playing racquetball. She and I played for an hour every week. What usually happened was that we'd play for a little while and then stand in the middle of the court and talk and talk and talk. Now, some people might say that was a waste of court time. Yet Mom and I would say it was relationship-building time. What really mattered was spending time together. Mom has taught me that good relationships take time, energy, and work, but they are well worth it.

"I" is for interdependent. I have seen my mom's and dad's relationship as one of interdependence. They depend on the Lord and each other to fulfill together and separately that which He has called them to do. They are perfectly comfortable with the gifts God has given each of them and they encourage each other to be all that he or she should be. Greg, my husband, and I have that kind of relationship as well. I am thankful to have grown up with that kind of a model for marriage.

"E" is for encourager. My mom always knows what to say in a given situation. She has a way with words. I meet people all over the world who can remember specific talks Mom gave years earlier because of her creative descriptions. One of the phrases that has helped me during these years as a mom of preschoolers is, "there are seasons of your life." Now that may sound basic, but it's something I have held onto as I've struggled with balancing family, ministry, and career. There will be seasons in my life when I may focus on one more fully than the others, or I may give each equal weight. The point is, whatever solution may work for today may not work for tomorrow because the season and circumstances might change.

I have been able to listen to Mom's descriptions of how she balanced taking care of three small children, running a nursery school, and working with teenagers. Listening to how this combination varied, depending on different situations, has helped me figure out the best balance for me at any given moment. I am confident that I am doing what I am supposed to be doing during whatever season I happen to be going through.

"N" is for Nanna. This is what my children call my mom. My mom is a teacher of my children. She loves to sit on my bed with my three boys and read to them. And she comes up with the most creative games. The kids love them. Sometimes, in the middle of the everyday chaos of car pools, T-ball, and laundry, I forget about the importance of spending quality time with my kids. Again, my mom becomes my teacher and reminds me of this important principle.

"D" is for determined. One of the reasons my mom is who she is today is because when she sets her mind to something, she does it. She is willing to try things she hasn't done before, even when she doesn't know whether she will succeed or not. Over the years, she has taught me that if there is something I believe God wants me to do, I should go for it, even if it might seem like a faraway goal.

Mom has encouraged me to be determined about my goals. Then she has been my personal cheerleader. When I was finishing my Ph.D., I found myself burning out. I would call my parents (or they would call me) very frequently just to hear a few words of encouragement. Basically, Mom and Dad would tell me they believed in me and they knew I could do it. This motivated me to finish the job.

Over the years, my mom has been my friend. She has taught me how to be that same kind of friend to others.

Dr. Judy Briscoe Golz is a psychologist, writer, speaker, and a leader in her church. She is also a visiting professor at Trinity Evangelical Divinity School in Deerfield, Illinois. Judy and her mother, Jill Briscoe, have an active speaking ministry as a mother-daughter team and have co-authored three books together.

CHAPTER THIRTEEN

WHEN FARTHER AWAY MEANT CLOSER
by Jane Kirkpatrick

I had lived within fifteen minutes of my mother for the last nine years of my marriage. Now, we were moving to rural Oregon and I would be three hours away. As I packed for the move, I began to feel some regrets when it came to my relationship with her.

For example, I wished I'd reached out to her more often, arrived at her house with a surprise picnic basket all planned for the two of us. I wished I'd invited my mom out for lunch—written her into my appointment calendar as I did my meetings at work.

But I hadn't and now, here I was, about to move away from her. What I didn't know at the time was that in the next few weeks, while staying in my parents' home until we finished our jobs and could move to our new location, I would grow closer to my mom than ever before.

It wasn't that I hadn't wanted closeness with my mom before. It was just that emotionally, we were miles apart. She was not one to frequently voice her love to me, at the most sometimes mumbling, "Love you, too," when I said, "I love you, Mom." And I always seemed to bungle my few attempts to get to know her better. Once I questioned her about her career—for years she had worked as a head nurse in a home for the elderly. But I must have sounded like a one-woman interrogation team instead of an interested party.

"It was hard," was all Mom had replied, shrugging her thin shoulders.

I felt the sadness of lost opportunity. If I couldn't get to know my mother when we had lived so close, how would I ever get to know her when I lived more than 100 miles away?

My parents left for a long-deserved vacation back east while we house-sat for them. Even though Mom was not physically present, I felt her presence all around me—when I watched TV from her comfy chair and fixed dinner in her pots and pans. But it was at church the following Sunday that I really got to know my mom.

I knew Mom was deeply dedicated to her church fellowship. That morning, sitting there in the old, sparsely furnished building that housed the little congregation, I saw how dedicated the members of the fellowship were to both my mom and my dad. After a rousing rendition of "Sunshine in My Soul," the pastor flipped on his tape recorder and said, "You all know Chuck and Pearl Rutschow are away from us for a few weeks. So let's all tell them how much we miss them." With that, everyone in the circle, including a dozen or so young parents, enthusiastically greeted my parents and offered special prayers for their health and safe return.

"I sure do miss your mom when she's gone," an older woman said to me later as we set silverware out for the after-church potluck. "She is such a blessing, and so faithful. If it weren't for her, I'd stand out like a sore thumb among all these young people."

I wondered about the special relationship between this elderly woman and my mom.

As I placed my mom's blue casserole dish on the table for the potluck, another woman spied it. "That dish looks very familiar. Your mom brought me dinner in it once, just after we'd moved into town. We ate from that casserole for three days. What a gift your mother offered to us—a family of complete strangers."

The potluck ended and I helped clean up, chatting with another woman about our upcoming move—the changes and adjustments it would bring.

"Your mom helped me move when I left here a year ago," she said. "She packed boxes for me and then your parents drove my daughter and me the 125 miles over the mountains to our new home. After that they visited us every few weeks. One weekend they showed up when I was so depressed. Your mother asked me how I was doing. Just knowing how much she cared, well, it was what kept me going. And then, a few months ago, when I felt so strongly that the Lord wanted us to move back here, it was your parents who were willing to come help me again as we trucked all our stuff back over the mountains."

I thought a lot about Mom during the next week. I found myself remembering little instances when she'd walked beside me and shared herself with me and my family.

I remembered the time I was sick and home from work. Mom arrived unexpectedly to fix dinner for the family and hot soup for me. Another time, while I was visiting my husband in the hospital, my mother cleaned my house and did my laundry. On and on the examples went—times when my mother had gifted me with her love.

The next Sunday, when we returned to the little church and the pastor asked if there were any blessings to share, I raised my hand.

"This whole week has been a special blessing for me," I said. "It began last Sunday during church. It isn't often that you get to see someone you love through other people's eyes. Thank you for helping me see the kind and generous person my mother is. The trouble was, I'd been too close to her to see it. But I'm thankful the Lord showed me through you all, and that he has allowed me to live long enough to appreciate my mother while she's still alive." I sat down, tears burning my eyes.

It was that lesson of my mother's love—not always spoken through words, but made clear through her deeds of kindness to me—that helped sustain me during the many changes and adjustments of a move. That move brought me closer to my mom and helped me realize what I'd had in her all along.

Jane Kirkpatrick is an author and speaker. Her novel, *A Sweetness to the Soul*, was voted Outstanding Western Novel of 1995 by the National Cowboy Hall of Fame and Western Heritage Center. Jane's other books include *Love to Water My Soul* and *Homestead*. She lives with her husband, Jerry, in a remote part of Eastern Oregon where she ranches and is a consultant to Native American communities. Jane's mother, Pearl Rutschow, is a retired nurse living in Sisters, Oregon, where she and her husband continue to touch others with their love.

CHAPTER FOURTEEN

A CARPET OF TRILLIUMS
by Louise Ferrebee

Slightly more than a decade ago, on a hot, humid August day, I said a final good-bye to my mother. Her seven-year duel with cancer was over. As I walked away from the grave site, I couldn't imagine how life would go on. Yet it did. Plenty of markers in my life prove just that.

Our home, which my mother saw only once—a few months after my husband, Tom, and I moved into it—was barely furnished. Today, it's completely decorated and we couldn't possibly squeeze another piece of furniture into it. The den and guest bedroom have long since been converted to havens for our two boys—grandsons my mother never knew.

The dishes Tom and I picked when we registered for wedding gifts and my mother ate off when she visited, have long since broken and been replaced (twice). Friends I once talked about in letters to my mother have moved on and new ones have filled their spots. Tom has changed jobs twice and I, once. There's little in my everyday world to connect me with a mother who saw me through my childhood and teenager years and left me just as I entered adulthood. And with less and less to tie her life with my present life, I slowly moved from missing her to desperately wanting to remember her. I looked around my world for some type of connection.

We'd never bought some special token to commemorate a memorable mother/daughter shopping spree. Materialistic pursuits never interested my mother. Trips to the store weren't for enjoyment but instead to "get the necessities." And besides that, as a young woman trying to establish my autonomy, my independent streak squelched any hopes of my asking her opinion on any purchase—even my wedding gown.

My paternal grandmother's collection of glassware and china fills my shelves and cupboards. Wherever I turn, I'm reminded of her. But not so with my mother. She never had a passion for one particular object and therefore didn't leave a collection of anything for me to continue to build upon.

We shared no common love for music, the arts, or literature. I remembered once asking her about an author she loved. Yet when I opened the pages of a novel by the same author, I couldn't get beyond the first chapter. I returned the book to its spot on the shelf and there it sat as a reminder of how little my mother and I seemed to have in common.

Discouraged that there appeared to be no shared love that would forever connect my thoughts to her, I resigned myself to the fact that my memories of her would continue to fade with each passing year. My quiet longing for some sense of connectedness would remain just that. Or so I thought.

Until several years ago, while driving home from a long weekend in northern Wisconsin, I spotted a blanket of trilliums covering the forest floor and spilling over on to the roadside.

"Stop the car!" I yelled to my husband, and then I bounded out the door with my camera in hand. I snapped a few shots, hoping I could capture the details of this delicate three-petal wildflower, so subtly etched with scarlet. "My mother loved these flowers, just look at them—hundreds and hundreds!" I said to Tom as I slammed the car door shut.

As the miles passed, memories of my mother popped into my mind.

"You must come on a walk with me to Vit's woods," I recalled her plea to me—a disinterested teenager. "The trilliums are out and they only last a short while. We should go see them."

So together we strolled to the woods a few blocks from our home. The sight was breathtaking. Under the filtered light of tall hardwood trees were trilliums as far as I could see.

My mind traveled to a similar encounter—this time in the woods of northern Michigan. The search was on for the illusive Lady's Slipper, a protected and exquisite wildflower. How my mother ever found one, I'll never know. Squatting down among the leafy ferns, I watched as she pulled back the dense cover of the forest floor to reveal a perfectly-shaped pink Lady's Slipper.

When my family returned from Wisconsin later that evening, I searched my bookshelves for a housewarming gift my mother had given me years earlier. Back then, *Crockett's Flower Garden* by Jim Crockett was a gift I graciously accepted but saw very little use for. The pages and pages on flowers seemed overwhelming to a new homeowner who was more worried about her kitchen wallpaper than her outside garden.

Now, for the first time, I paged through the thick, colorful book my mother had given me. I challenged myself to see if I could identify a plant without first reading the photo caption.

To my surprise, a connection was growing—one I had entirely missed in my search to establish a tie with my mother. My mother was a botanist. The outdoors—the living world of plants—was her passion. She had even discovered and named a new plant in the California desert during her college days at Stanford University. The connection I so desired and was looking for had, until then, been only on my terms, dictated by my interest. Now, the connection was on her terms. I felt a growing love for, and interest in, plants.

I looked at my yard and garden in a new light. What I didn't realize was that in all the years of growing up with my mother, she had somehow managed to plant in my heart a love for gardening and the outdoors, and when the time was ripe that seed would germinate and grow. In the days ahead, I was amazed as I watched my interest in gardening and plants take root—not out of a sense of dedication to my mother's memory but from the same source of pure joy she once must have experienced.

When the chance came to dig up several of the day lilies that bloomed in the garden she had once tended, I quickly grabbed a shovel and transplanted the clumps 280 miles south to my home. Today, with each golden orange bloom that bursts forth in the heat of July, I'm reminded of her. And like her, I find myself pouring through seed catalogues in the dead of winter with dreams of spring planting. Or, dragging my children to Frank's Nursery for potting soil, perennials, and tools. Even last week, I had to laugh when I asked my family, "Who took my favorite trowel?" My mother's words exactly—only as a child I certainly didn't see the difference between one shovel or another. I'm even considering paying my boys a penny for every weed they pick, the same pretext my mother used to get me in the garden.

Within the next few weeks, colorful zinnias will blossom again in my garden. I'll be outside, scissors in hand and fighting mosquitoes, to clip a few for a kitchen table bouquet. And there, in the center of my table will be a fresh reminder of my mother and I'll smile each time I pass by the table. I know now, with certainty, memories of my mother won't fade but instead will come back stronger and stronger each year in the language of living plants.

I doubt I'll ever know as much about plants as my mother did, but the excitement lies in the realization I have a lifetime to learn. And with each new discovery or lesson, I'm drawn closer to her memory. She passed along to me the love of God's creation, and in the process she passed on a connection between us that can't be broken, wear out, or be taken away. She knew, as I am also learning, to love more what God has created and less what man has created. I could not value a lesson more.

Louise Ferrebee is an associate editor with *Marriage Partnership Magazine*. She currently lives in Wheaton, Illinois. Her mother, Mary Louise Hammack, was a school teacher who grew up in southern Indiana.

CHAPTER FIFTEEN

THE INVESTMENT OF A LIFETIME
by Vonette Zachary Bright

No woman has had a greater influence on my life than Mary Margaret Waggoner Zachary. Mother taught me, by word and example, that being a woman was a great calling. Never did I entertain the thought that being a woman made me a second-class citizen or limited me in anything. Nor did it occur to me, thanks to my mother's input, that I was to compete with a man. Rather, I was a compliment to men, and they to me.

As my two brothers and I were growing up, Mother encouraged our personal development and our achievements. She saw that we had lessons of various kinds. We started taking lessons in tap dancing at the age of two and four years. Later came speech, piano, voice, water color and oil painting. As a result, I have developed a great interest in art, music, dance, and literature.

Most of all, mother was always right there, helping to make our development happen. One of my earliest recollections is of standing on the platform of our small-town Oklahoma church, practicing a four-line rhyme to give at the Sunday school "opening exercises."

I can still see my mother, standing at the back of the sanctuary as I practiced, holding her hand to her ear, saying, "I can't hear you. Speak loudly." She helped me with everything—how to walk to the platform, how to stand, how to speak, and then how to sit down again. When the time came for my part in the program, I felt much more confident because Mother had spent time helping me prepare.

When my brother Glenn and I were small, Dad worked as an automobile salesman in a Ford car agency. Many times he returned home late in the evening. In order for us to be able to spend time with Dad, Mother allowed us to stay up late. She saw to it that we slept late in the morning and napped in the afternoon. She planned nightly performances for us to entertain him. Sometimes we quoted nursery rhymes, recited simple poetry, sang songs, tap danced, or demonstrated some of our accomplishments from the day. This became a much anticipated nightly ritual.

Mother and Daddy always said their greatest investment was in their children. When we were small, they seldom, if ever, left us alone or with a baby-sitter. Their activities centered around activities we could do as a family. As we got older, our home was always a gathering place for kids our age. Mother sort of grew up with her children and our friends loved to have her around. My parents gave us lots of liberty within boundaries. They didn't give us much opportunity to get out of hand because they provided so much fun at home; we didn't have to go elsewhere to find it.

I remember when our house had been newly decorated, about the same time one of my brothers and I were learning ballroom dancing. We wanted to have a party where we could dance. Mother said, "Okay. You can wax the garage floor and dance there."

But by the end of the evening she felt badly that the party was not in the house. The next party we wanted to give, up came the carpets and we held the dance in the house. The only requirement Mother made was that we had to wax and polish the pinewood floors before and after the party. We didn't mind. We recruited all our friends and waxing the floors was as much fun as the party. Mother liked us to entertain at home. That way she knew where we were and what we were doing.

Soon after my second brother was born, my father became extremely ill with pneumonia and typhoid fever. Without the antibiotics of today, just one of those illnesses alone could be life threatening. Dr. Riddle, our small-town doctor, gave Mother careful instructions on how to care for Dad at home. I remember her preparing chicken in a jar placed in boiling water. She did it, she said, to give Dad the pure undiluted broth from the chicken. She light-heartedly referred to the broth as "the Jewish Mama's penicillin."

During this time Dad had been managing our town's major grocery store and meat market. Just as he was recuperating from his lengthy illness and was almost ready to go back to work, the widow of the man who had hired Dad came to our house one Sunday morning. She informed Dad that his services at the grocery store were no longer needed.

I remember that was a dark day. I was seven and my brothers were six and two. I can still see my parents talking about what to do.

Mother was courageous and encouraging. She asked Dad if he could manage the children and the house for a while and she would go back to the post office job she'd had before they'd been married. So my Dad stayed home with the children for a while and my mother became Assistant Postmaster. (The only reason she didn't become Postmaster was that she was of the wrong political party!)

I had my favorite birthday of all my growing up years during the time that Dad was home with us kids. He gave the party. Mom baked the cake but Dad made homemade ice cream—the kind you make with an old hand-cranked freezer. I still have pictures of that party. They are among my most treasured pictures.

Mother was very frugal during those days when money was tight. Those were post-Depression days and despite the fact she'd married when she was only seventeen, Mother had learned to manage well. She wrote down every penny she spent. It wasn't too long before Dad bought a filling station business and Mother became a "stay-at-home-mom" again.

As we got older, she became active in the Church Missionary Society, serving as President for several years. She also volunteered to be the Church Treasurer, which required keeping track of the weekly offering envelopes and paying the church bills. She joined the local "Study Club", which is affiliated with the National Federation of Women's Clubs. It was there that she became aware of many issues that were affecting the home and family—inspiring an even greater interest in political matters. Later, she held several local, district, and state offices in the Women's Club organization.

When World War II began and women were encouraged to work for the war effort, many women from our town went to Tulsa to work in defense factories. Dad had a hard time getting adequate help, so Mother began managing his office and posting his books. When business was heavy and Dad was alone, she even filled gas tanks and wiped windshields. After the war, her job with Dad was no longer full-time, but she still posted his books.

Mother firmly believed that our teachable moments as children were when we were working on tasks together. As a teenager, seldom was I left to wash dishes, clean house, or prepare a meal alone. Mother worked with me and it was during those times I began to confide in her. She became my best friend. We talked about boys, dress, dating, goal-setting, relationships with friends, marriage, and plans for my future.

"Never date a person you would not marry," she would say to me. Or, "Don't marry a person who's faults overshadow his good points." Somehow, I never felt I was receiving lectures. Mother was only sharing her perspectives with me.

Mom was always awake when I came home from a date and was willing to listen to my rehearsal of all the details. Did I have fun? Who were we with? What did they wear? Sometimes we would talk into the wee hours of the morning.

Mother was always one to be learning something new. As my younger sister was getting older, Mother enrolled in a Toastmistress Club. Public speaking was something she had always wanted to learn. After Dad passed away, she enrolled in Tulsa Junior College. She ended up on the Dean's Honor Roll.

Even today, well into her senior years (she tells us, "You are only as old as you feel," or "Any woman who will tell her age will tell anything!"), she still is learning. She loves mind-challenging games. When she comes to stay with us, some of my friends come to see me just so they can play games with Mother.

Mother refuses to get old. She had to be in a therapy class two years ago because of an injured shoulder. Even there, she was the star patient, surprising everyone with her discipline in the exercises. Needless to say, she made a rapid recovery.

I have been handed a great legacy by my mother. She has given me life, love, security, confidence, encouragement, companionship, advice, reverence for God. It wasn't until I visited, for the first time as an adult, my grandmother's grave, that I felt the true impact of my mother's life. The words carved on my grandmother's tombstone were, "She died as she lived, trusting in Jesus." My grandmother's trust was honored, for her children and her grandchildren are all committed Christians. What greater legacy could a child ask for?

Vonette Zachary Bright is the co-founder (along with her husband, Dr. William Bright) of Campus Crusade for Christ International, which began in 1951. She was also a founding member and the chairman of the National Prayer Committee, which helped pass legislation in the United States to make the first Thursday of each May the National Day of Prayer. Mrs. Bright has authored several books, her most recent being *The Joy of Hospitality.* Vonette's mother, Mary Margaret Waggoner Zachary, lives in Oklahoma and frequently travels with Vonette and her husband in their ministry around the world.

CHAPTER SIXTEEN

FAITH IS...

...CONFIDENCE IN GOD'S FAITHFULNESS TO ME IN AN UNCERTAIN WORLD, OR AN UNCHARTED COURSE, TOWARD AN UNKNOWN FUTURE.

by Pamela Reeve

When I wrote the little book, *Faith Is...*, I gave one of the first copies to my mother. I wrote in it:

To Mother,
Whose life
chapter by chapter
has been the best commentary
on faith
I have ever read.

The chapters in my mother's life were far from easy. Her father died when she was nine, her husband when she was forty-eight. For four of my growing up years she cared for her bed-ridden mother, and for four more years she cared for my very ill father. We went through the Great Depression of 1929 and suffered severe financial losses. She was deeply hurt by a family problem but refused to hold any bitterness—continually moving out in love to the offender.

At seventy-five she had a massive heart attack. The doctor said that only two things pulled her through—she had no fear of death and she had "a merry heart." Several heart attacks and eight years later, she died. On the morning of her death she wrote in her diary, "God is good." They were the last words she wrote.

Mother was of the old school—she rarely moralized and was never "preachy." Her life simply radiated deep joy and contentment. She left the clear impression in my mind that God was wise, that he was good and that he could be trusted.

Her understanding and compassion knew no bounds. A homey incident on the animal level illustrates this. Mother lived with me and after her heart problems she wasn't allowed to drive and so was alone all day and many weekends when I was at work—especially hard for a people lover. Her dearly-loved cat "Peng Dee" was her constant companion those long hours I was gone.

One Saturday when I was home, Peng Dee was chased by Sheba, a cat known to all in the neighborhood as a very mean cat. In the ensuing chase, mother's beloved Peng Dee was killed by a car. A neighbor came to console my mother.

"You should just kill that Sheba," the neighbor said. "Just kill her."

My mother's instant reply didn't surprise me. "If you understood Sheba's problems you wouldn't hold it against her." Sheba lived in the home of an alcoholic who often kicked and abused her. Mother could look beyond her own pain and keep loving.

Mother's response to people was the same. She never judged by outward appearances. She loved the unlovely—the porcupine people— and listened to what was going on in their hearts. She was one of the most understanding and compassionate persons I've known.

For mother, life was about giving of herself to others, and this was the mind set she gave me. Others remember my mother for her love of life, her broad interests, her delight in the simplest of things. I remember her most for the way she molded my attitudes toward God, people and life. As she wrote in her diary the day she died—and on my heart-—God *is* good.

Dr. Pamela Reeve is a popular author, conference speaker, and professor at Multnomah Biblical Seminary in Portland, Oregon. Her books include *Faith Is...*, which has sold more than one million copies. Pam's mother, Ethel Reeve, grew up in Brooklyn and served as President for both the local Red Cross chapter and the Hospital Auxiliary. She founded and directed the women's ministry at her church and was among the first to march for the voting rights of women.

CHAPTER SEVENTEEN

MOTHER'S MEAT LOAF NEVER EXPLODED
(AND OTHER TALENTS I DID NOT GET FROM MY MOTHER)
by Martha Bolton

I'm happy to say I did not get my talent for kitchen disasters from my mother. My mother was a wonderful cook. *Her* meat loaf never exploded. *Her* homemade dinner rolls were never used as decorative rocks for landscaping. *She* never had to add Rolaids instead of chocolate chips to her cookie recipe. I can't recall one single kitchen fire or ptomaine-related trip to the emergency room. Everything she baked, broiled, fried, or microwaved turned out perfectly. My children, on the other hand, grew up thinking clouds were *supposed* to be inside the house.

My mother also had a beautiful voice. I didn't inherit that talent either. She tried her best to teach me to sing, but her instructions fell on deaf ears (which is where most people say my singing should fall).

The value of hard work, though, is something I hope I did learn from my mother. If I didn't, it wasn't for lack of an example. At seventy-two, she was well on her way to her third retirement. Over the years, the building where she worked was bought out by two other companies. As soon as one company retired my mother, she would be hired to work for the new one. It was as if she came with the building, as though she were named in escrow.

Not only was my mother a professional, she also found time to be involved in PTA, serving as president and even moving up to one of the district offices. She worked at the school on her day off and attended evening meetings, and I don't recall either of my parents ever missing an open house (since I'm the youngest of five children, that's a lot of open houses!).

As busy as she was, you'd think she'd take Sundays off. She didn't. She made sure we attended Sunday school, Sunday morning worship, and Sunday evening services every week (with plenty of Wednesday night services thrown in, too). And we're not talking about a neighborhood church either. We'd drive twenty miles one way to attend church. With five kids, there was hardly any room in our car for more, but somehow my mother always found a way to squeeze in one or two of our friends (and that was in the day before minivans!).

Raised in church herself, my mother had a gentle spirituality. She never preached at anyone or stood up on a soapbox. She merely did her best to live what the Bible said, and she knew who to lean on through the tough times in life.

Aside from her example of faith, what I value most about my mother was her sense of humor. She loved to laugh. No matter what amount of stress she was under, it was never more than her sense of humor could bear. In fact, her sense of humor seemed to abound in times of trouble.

I married at eighteen and never lived more than a few miles from my parents. We lived so close, Mom could step out onto her front porch, take a whiff, and know what I was burning that night for dinner. Even living that close, though, I still felt a need to spend more time with my mother, especially after the death of my father. We tend to think our parents will always be there, waiting for that time when our calendars are a little less hectic. Sadly, that isn't always the case.

I began taking my mother for weekend trips. My husband graciously volunteered to watch our sons, and I'd "kidnap" Mom and whisk her away for a few days of pure fun. My mother had always dreamed of visiting Washington, DC, so one weekend we flew from LAX to our nation's capitol. I had a limo waiting to meet her, but when my mother saw the elderly driver dressed in a suit, smiling at us with a toothless grin and a sign bearing her last name, she refused to take another step until I assured her he wasn't a blind date. That was the first of many laughs we shared that weekend.

Shortly after her seventy-second birthday, Mom was diagnosed with lymphoma and given three weeks to live unless chemotherapy was started right away. Mom had hardly been sick a day in her life, and at first she denied the cancer. After a biopsy, a bone marrow test and numerous blood tests and x-rays, she eventually came to terms with the illness. She then focused all of her attention on beating it. She almost did, too. She lived another eight months, finally succumbing the day before Mother's Day.

I know I'll never be the cook my mother was or sing as well as she could, but I hope I inherited her positive outlook on life, her drive, and even a fraction of her heart.

Martha Bolton has a long history of laughter—she has worked as a staff writer for Bob Hope, the head writer for *The Mark and Kathy Show*, and a writer for Mark Lowry. She is also the winner of two Angel Awards and was an Emmy Award nominee. She has twenty-three books to her credit, including *When the Going Gets Tough, the Tough Starts Laughing*, and *Who Put the Pizza in the VCR?* Her mother, Eunice Delores Ella Ferren, was a department store buyer in southern California. Martha and her mom enjoyed doing many things together, including "traveling, sightseeing, shopping, and *laughing!*"

CHAPTER EIGHTEEN

MORE BONES THAN SOUP:
A LESSON IN THANKFULNESS
by *Martha Reapsome*

A bowl of soup made from the neck bones of a turkey taught me a childhood lesson I've never forgotten. When Daddy, a paper-hanger, fell off a ladder and broke his back, Mother took a job as a cook in a local hotel. She was grateful for any discards she could use from the hotel kitchen. One night when Mother served turkey soup made from neck bones, I wailed with all the disdain only a six-year-old could muster: "There are more bones than soup. I can't eat this."

Mother responded sharply, "Be thankful you have something to eat."

Mother's rebuke over that turkey soup still stimulates my sense of thankfulness. I do not journal daily, but I do keep a "Thank You Journal" for at least monthly entries. It forces me to recall and reflect on God's faithfulness and presence in my life and those around me. Rereading the accounts of God's goodness leads me to trust him more.

Mother's thankful spirit often overflowed into song. As she worked in the kitchen, she sang from her large repertoire of hymns: *Amazing Grace, What a Wonderful Savior, What a Friend We Have in Jesus.* Because she was thankful, she willingly gave of what she had. I often heard her and Daddy discussing the decision they'd made before they married, that they would take a tithe of 10 percent out of each of Daddy's paychecks. Mother reminded me often, "Look how God has provided for us—the good food, a house, everything we need." As a child, the point was clear: God cares for us. Not to love and honor him in return would be foolish.

Mother's thankful spirit led her to give not only from her money but from her gifts and abilities as well. She was always teaching Sunday school, serving as Sunday school superintendent, serving on the church board or inviting people to church. The pastor once commented about my mother, "When someone is moving into our area, Ella follows the moving van into town and invites the people to church."

Growing up, it never occurred to me that Christian women would not use their spiritual gifts, talents and time to serve Jesus in the church and the community. I saw that godly women can be strong and still have "the unfading beauty of a gentle and quiet spirit which is of great worth in God's sight" (1 Peter 3:4).

When I sensed God's call to a full-time Christian vocation, my parents were delighted. In our church, I had never met a missionary. But when Mother learned that Margaret Shepherd, a missionary to India, was coming to another church in Louisville, she somehow arranged for Margaret to visit our church and, of course, to have dinner with us. Years later, God directed me to the staff of InterVarsity Christian Fellowship instead of overseas. In contrast to my aunt, who protested that since I was single I should stay and care for my aging, ailing parents, Mother rejoiced in my opportunity to serve Jesus and students in Ohio.

Mother's thankful spirit helped to make our home a place of loving hospitality. What happy childhood memories I have of several families enjoying potluck get-togethers after church. The teenage friends of my older siblings were always filling our porch or living room. We often had one or more boarders in the house to supplement Daddy's paper-hanging business. Some boarders were easier to live with than others, but each received respect and love from Mother.

Mother was always looking for ways to share what she had. In the '30s, when the Work Project Administration (a federal program to provide jobs to the unemployed) workers rebuilt the road past our farm, Mother carried hot coffee and freshly baked kuchen from the house to the garage where the men took refuge from the cold. One neighbor chided, "Mrs. Gray, those men won't ever finish the road past your farm if you keep feeding them!"

Mother also shared with our friends. Each of us children brought home friends who became like adopted brothers and sisters. Many of them found this hugging, loving home a totally new experience. One friend said, "As I walk up the steps to your house, the love flows out from the front door." Seeing Daddy sitting on the sofa, holding hands with his "sweetheart" of forty-plus years conveyed to my friends more than words ever could about love and loyalty between husband and wife.

Today, my husband Jim and I pray that our home will be a place of such love and peace that everyone who enters will feel welcome and loved. Whether we share a cup of coffee, a bowl of popcorn, a potluck supper or a celebration dinner, the guests are the focus. At different times, God has given us special friendships with single adults, some who have never seen a Christian home. Just being ourselves and including them in Tuesday night supper has enriched us and them.

My mother's spirit of thanksgiving lasted all her life. One day, when Mother was dying after two years as a semi-invalid, she asked my sister and me, "Do you think I have been guilty of unthankfulness?" She knew the Bible's warning about those who did not give thanks. My sister and I assured her we were confident lack of gratitude was one sin of which she was not guilty.

Today, I pray that I will be as faithful in using the multitude of resources God has given me as my mother was in using hers. I pray I will continue the spirit of thanksgiving she lived out as an example before me.

Martha Reapsome is Midwest Director of Neighborhood Bible Studies, and author of several books such as *The Journey of a Lifetime and Growing through Life's Challenges*, both published by Shaw. Her mother, Ella Thompson Gray, was a homemaker, Sunday school teacher and church leader.

CHAPTER NINETEEN

"THE KING IS COMING" AND OTHER MEMORIES OF MOTHER
by Ruth Bell Graham

My mother, Virginia Meyers Leftwich Bell, was of sturdy Virginian stock. Among her relatives were a Princeton historian and a librarian of the University of Virginia in Thomas Jefferson's day. She and my father had attended the same high school in Waynesboro, Virginia, were together on the tennis team, dramatic club, the literary society, and the choir. My father was an outstanding baseball player (even playing professionally for a while), and I'm told his favorite line was, "Where's Virginia?" From the earliest high school days on, my mother was always in the stands, encouraging my father on.

It was her way of life. When my father, who was at Washington and Lee University studying pre-law, heard God's call to be a missionary doctor, my mother gave whole-hearted support. They were engaged at the time so she knew his decision would have ramifications on her for the rest of her life. And when they sailed for China five years later, she went willingly, yes, gladly.

During their twenty-five years of medical work at the Love and Mercy Hospital in Tsingkiangpu, China, Mother was right there by my father's side. In the early years she ran the hospital's housekeeping department, helped in the dispensary, and assisted during operations. Later, as she served in the hospital and became more and more acquainted with the diseases and how to treat them, she took responsibility for all the women patients, leaving only the sickest ones for my father to see. My father often said he'd rather have Virginia in his department at the hospital than another doctor.

The years my parents served in China, from 1916 to 1941, were tumultuous years for the country. Chaos and disorder reigned. Warlords ruled the provinces. Bandits roamed the country, terrorizing the citizens. Later years brought the Japanese invasion when Japanese bombers flew so low over our house we could see writing on the underbelly of the planes. Even though we were often surrounded by great danger, and the government, it seemed, was always sending orders for at least my mother and us children to evacuate, my mother refused to leave my father's side. She decided early on that whatever dangers there were, all the Bells would share those dangers together. She stood by that decision through many tense moments when others had fled the city for safety in the countryside. If Daddy was determined to stay by the hospital and his patients, Mother was right there with him.

One of the things I remember most about my mother was the way she stood by my father. Years later, when I became the wife of Billy Graham, it was much easier for me because I'd seen in my mother what support for a husband was all about.

From my mother, I also learned about gracious "good-byes." My father was often off into the countryside to treat medical needs. Sometimes he was gone for long periods of time. Of course, I didn't know it at the time, but God was preparing me for a lifetime of good-byes. Even though each time Billy left for a crusade it felt like a "small death" (as I once wrote in a poem), the good-byes were much easier because I'd seen my mother having to say so many good-byes—not only to her husband but to my sisters and me when we went away to high school in Korea and then on to college in America.

Another thing I remember vividly about my mother was she always made our home a fun place to be. Both my parents had a great sense of humor and loved to play games. When Daddy died, at age seventy-nine, he and Mother were still playing a game of Scrabble almost every night. When I was growing up, there was always some kind of celebration going on at our house with the other missionaries—from birthday parties to baby showers. We celebrated all the American holidays with great flourish. Our house was always open to missionaries who were passing through or new recruits. One young doctor and his wife lived with us nearly a year until a house was available for them. Mother never seemed put out or bothered by this. She received guests with open arms.

One of my favorite times was when the missionaries on our compound, and the neighboring compound met each week for game night. I can remember the fun we children had as we ran around the yard playing—the grownups' laughter ringing through the night. Rook was the favorite game for the adults, and later my father even figured out a way to create a miniature golf course in our yard. Mother went out of her way to make sure that every person felt comfortable and at home. Outside the compound, there would be gunfire, raids, and looting. But inside was a place of laughter, light-heartedness, and fun.

If my mother was afraid, she never showed it. She was probably the most courageous woman I have ever known. Even during the Japanese invasion, when my mother would be sitting with my younger brother and sister in the air-raid shelter that Daddy had fixed up for the family out of a concrete water cistern, she seemed calm and perfectly at peace. Although I was away at college at the time, I'm told she and Daddy would sing and quote scripture about God's protection. Many times, she and Daddy were the last to evacuate a city when there was trouble, and always Mother would be the one encouraging Daddy to stay on. Throughout all the danger of our years in China, Mother communicated her calm to us children. I don't remember being afraid. In fact, we children usually looked at the unrest around us as a sort of adventure. I'm sure that had a great deal to do with my mother's attitude.

Years after my parents had left China, at a Family Life Conference in Montreat, North Carolina, where my parents had settled, Mother was honored for her "patience and help" to my father. She was in her eighties by then, had suffered a stroke and was confined to a wheelchair. But that day, the entire audience of three thousand stood and applauded my mother.

And when, months later at the age of 82, we knew she was in her final days, her one desire was to have us play the song, "The King is Coming" on her little cassette player. I'm confident she joined the ranks of heaven with great applause and with God's words "well done" ringing loudly in her ears.

Ruth Bell Graham is the wife of evangelist Billy Graham and the author of seven books, including *One Wintery Night* and *Prodigals* and *Those Who Love Them*. She has raised five children, loves old things, and lives in a house she had constructed from old mountain log cabins. Her mother, Virginia Bell, died in 1974.

CHAPTER TWENTY

MOTHERS TOGETHER
by Gigi Grahm Tchividjian

My heart flooded with pride as I took my seat next to Stephen. I placed child number seven (not quite five years old) on the other side of me—close enough to grab or pinch, whichever became necessary first. I glanced down the pew and chuckled to see that Stephen, myself, and our children filled up the entire second row. All seven were dressed in their Sunday best. The boys looked so handsome, and the two girls were especially lovely on this day.

Following the call to worship, our pastor asked the men to come forward and kneel at the altar, dedicating themselves and the worship service to the Lord. I thought my heart would burst with gratitude as my five sons knelt beside their father. How blessed I was on this Mother's Day!

My thoughts drifted to what seemed like just a few short years ago. I was seventeen and a new bride living in Switzerland. A month after my wedding, when I discovered I was not "with child," I burst into tears thinking I would never have children. I am sure the Lord must have smiled, but he granted me "the desires of my heart" and ten months later our first son was born. I remembered the joy I felt as I celebrated that first Mother's Day as a mother.

My thoughts continued, recalling another Mother's Day a couple of years later.

I awoke that Sunday morning to the sound of bells. The valley was alive with them. The tinkling cow bells with the tolling church bells.

Opening the heavy wooden shutters covering the windows in our small chalet, I gazed in wonder at the beauty before me. It was one of those indescribable spring days that can only be experienced in the Alps. I took in a deep breath of the cool, crisp air rushing in through the open window. The early morning sun was just beginning to reflect off the snow-covered peaks surrounding our valley. The wild flowers strewn across the fields below were ready to burst into a riot of color...purple, yellow, blue, mauve.

I turned to look at my small son asleep in his crib, and felt the delicate movements of the unborn child within me. I was filled with warm emotion.

Slipping on my robe, I gently gathered my sleeping son in my arms. In the kitchen, I found my mother who had come to share this day with us. She had already made the cafe au lait and was slicing the thick, Swiss bread. As we sat together sipping the hot coffee and eating bread smothered with rich butter and strawberry jam, I was overwhelmed with joy.

Mother reached into her pocket and handed me an envelope. I opened it and discovered her Mother's Day gift to me.

It seems but yesterday
you lay
new in my arms.
Into our lives you brought
sunshine and laughter—
play—
showers, too,
and song.
Headstrong,
heart strong,
gay,
tender beyond believing,
simple in faith,
clear-eyed,
shy,
eager for life—
you left us

rich in memories,
little wife.
And now today
I hear you say
words beyond your years.
I watch you play
with your small son,
tenderest of mothers.
Years slip away—
today
we are mothers
together.
                    —Ruth Bell Graham

As I sat there beside my children in the pew, I couldn't help but reflect on how quickly the years had passed.

The small son I cradled that day is now a father with two little ones of his own. The unborn child that stirred within me is now a happily married woman. Several brothers and sisters followed them. And now Mother and I are not only mothers together, but grandmothers together.

Children so quickly grow into parents, parents into grandparents, and grandparents into great grandparents. The role of parenting, I thought to myself, is like the ever widening ripple a stone makes in the quiet waters of a mountain lake. Once you love, you are never free again.

I reflect on over twenty-six years of mothering, and I agree with what John Trapp said many years ago: "Children are certain cares, uncertain joys."

I smiled to myself. Although the joys have far outweighed the cares and parenthood continues to be my most rewarding occupation, I do not find it easy. Parenting is a huge responsibility. It is physically, emotionally, and spiritually demanding. I thought of how Satan is attacking today's families. I thought back on the past year and how he had attacked our family. At times, the circumstances seemed overwhelming.

But God, ever true to His word, always provided the needed strength and promised wisdom.

My mother was once asked how she had raised five children with my Daddy being away so much of the time.

"On my knees," she replied.

Certainly I had not discovered a better or more effective way to raise children.

We are all parents together, striving to be faithful with the responsibilities that God has entrusted to each of us. There are many times we feel overwhelmed or become discouraged. But God is a father with a mother's heart. When we feel depleted, we simply turn to him and exchange our insufficiency for his all-sufficiency.

With David we can say, "The Lord is my strength...my heart trusts in him, and I am helped" (Psalm 28:7).[1]

Gigi Graham Tchividjian is the wife of psychologist Stephen Tchividjian, mother of seven and grandmother of three. She is the oldest of five children. Her mother, Ruth Graham, is the wife of evangelist Billy Graham.

[1] Used with permission from *Weather of the Heart,* by Gigi Graham Tchividjian, Baker Book House, Grand Rapids, Michigan.

CHAPTER TWENTY-ONE

IS THIS CAR GOING TO VIRGINIA?
by Ruth Graham McIntyre

*H*ow do I see my mother?

As a woman of joy—like the living water that "shall be in her a well of water springing up into everlasting life."

Mother's parents had a profound effect on the development of her character. They laid the foundations for what and who she is. I observe traits in her now that I know were formed long ago by her godly parents who were committed to Christ and to their family. Early in Mother's life, Christ became her purpose.

One word that does not apply to my mother in any form is "condemnation." She has a marvelous capacity to accept people as they are. She stays in touch with an assortment of friends—from a London waif whom she has tried to nurture, to those of royal blood, to the mountain men who helped build our family house, to early childhood friends.

She has a strong sense of family and holds to traditions passed through the generations. She is happiest when she is in her home in the mountains of North Carolina surrounded by her husband and children and grandchildren, and her well-used books. Living, as I do, in Virginia under the shadow of the mountains that nurtured Mother's parents, I understand my feelings for being rooted.

My mother has never been tempted by status or by acquiring things, but old things have always appealed to her. They make her feel at home. In 1989 I accompanied her as she returned to China, where she had spent her childhood. I began to understand the source of her preferences. In Chinese culture old things and elderly people are revered. Mother absorbed that appreciation with her artistic sensitivity.

She is a collector of books, and through the years she has found some rare or unusual ones. She has never understood, however, why people collect books just to decorate a room. Her books are her friends. Her bedside is crowded with a variety of books and always, nearby, her beloved Bible.

When someone told her that he felt guilty if he started reading a second book before finishing the first, she told him that she doesn't feel guilty. "After all," she said, "you don't finish all the pickles before you eat the olives."

She sprinkles her conversation with statements of humor and understanding—sometimes outlandish, but never dull. She has a marvelous sense of the ridiculous.

Because she doesn't take herself seriously, she can laugh at herself. Several years ago she was driving up to stay with me for a few days. Having never driven to my home before, she was unsure of the way, but she noticed a little, red car with a Virginia license plate, so she just followed it. By the time that she got to Winston-Salem, North Carolina, she realized that the red car was not going to Virginia! Mother had gone one and a half hours out of her way. Some people might become uptight and frustrated. Not my mother! She was chuckling when she finally arrived—late but safe—at my home.

Mother has experienced sorrow, burdens, injustice, confusion, pressure, hurt, pain. Yet I have never seen her display anger or doubt. She has a tender and yielded heart. Her happiness and her fulfillment do not depend on her circumstances. I realize that she is the lovely, beautiful and wise woman who she is because early in her life she made Jesus Christ her home, her purpose, her center, her confidant, her vision.

I associate joy with my mother, and I understand now that "the joy of the Lord is her strength" and mine.[1]

Ruth Graham McIntyre is Donor Relations Coordinator for Samaritan's Purse. She is also the author of *First Steps in the Bible*, and a mother of three. She is one of five children. Her mother, Ruth Graham, is the wife of evangelist Billy Graham.

[1] This story taken with permission from "A Heart for the World: Ruth Bell Graham," by Ruth Graham McIntyre, in "Ambassadors for Christ, Distinguished Representatives of the Message Throughout the World" edited by John D. Woodbridge, Moody Bible Institute, Moody Press, Chicago, Illinois.

CHAPTER TWENTY-TWO

A QUART OF BLUEBERRIES AND
A TANK FULL OF LOVE
by Christine Wyrtzen

*S*omeone has wisely said, "The closest thing on earth to God's love for his children is a mother's love for hers." This adage was certainly true of my mother.

Perhaps my mother's richness of spirit was born in her own childhood—a time traced with pain and intense struggles. The unpredictable moods of her mentally ill father caused his wife and their seven children to live confined in a house of fear. The house itself was consumed by fire when Mother was only ten, and the following winter found the family huddled around a wood stove in a barn. The winters in Upstate New York can still bring a man to his knees. Little wonder my mother rarely spoke of her own childhood.

My mother was not formally educated beyond high school yet she held a responsible job with the New York State Health Department. She was respected for her quick mind, wit, and work ethic. Though her career ended when her children came, her passion for learning continued to foster her natural sense of curiosity. Her life was lived with a novel in one hand and a tool for grooming the nearby woods in the other. The books often chronicled the times and trials of those entrapped by World War II. In fact, her friends thought her to be a "walking encyclopedia" on matters of the War. Not one to leave a book on a shelf to collect dust, she took on the challenge of trying to correspond with one of the top Nazi officials and refused to let language be a barrier by first contacting a German interpreter. Certainly his time in the prison cell was made a bit more pleasant by the company of my mother's correspondence.

The harrowing first expeditions to the North Pole also captured my mother's imagination for hours on end. Mom would repeat tales at dinner and recount the ways men would literally tunnel through mountains to build much needed roads. Her voice would rise near the climax of the story as she would tell us of the perilous challenges they faced and the perseverance it took to gain victory. The thrill of conquering what seemed insurmountable seemed to give her a sense of resolve unlike that which her daily life offered. Perhaps that was part of her secret…the mystery of the tools she had used to survive those early childhood years.

With the grace and dignity of a natural dancer, she could sway with ease from one setting to another, whether sitting with a missionary group from church as she helped to make quilts for those abroad or conversing with a Ph.D. from a nearby university. A prepared sense of well-being seemed to accompany her, no matter what the occasion or with whom she was dining.

My mom certainly had the gift of friendship or, as the book of Romans calls it, "hospitality." She had a reputation throughout our town of 1200 for her trademark recipes—which always contained berries she had picked herself. During picking seasons, she made trips into Maine and even scoured the small mountain paths of the Taconic Mountains in upper New York to locate prize berries.

She froze the berries and they later found their way into her award-winning culinary creations. And then, she would give someone a delightful culinary experience while extending the hand of friendship with blueberry-stained fingers.

Whether using her own kitchen as a backdrop or seeking out someone who could use a friend, Mom was always extending a warm taste-treat that opened many, many conversations in that little mountain town in upper New York.

We still aren't sure if it's genetic or the result of imitation, but my husband Ron and I served homemade blueberry muffins to a couple new to God's family just this morning. They, like the many Mom served, needed someone to talk to about some of life's tough questions.

My mom consistently modeled a clear understanding of Ecclesiastes 4:9-12—"Two are better than one. If one falls down the other can help him up. If one is overpowered, two can defend themselves. If two lie down together, they shall be warm. A threefold chord cannot be easily broken."

Every town of any size has its "less than desirable citizens," and Petersburg, New York, was no exception. I remember two in particular— a town drunk and a strange old lady with the curtains always drawn. Mom reached out to them. They always knew they could call on her when a need arose. Winter time usually meant Mom would hear from many in need of coal for the wood stove or a trip into town for groceries. My mom willingly drove them. My sister and I could never understand how Mom could ride in the closed car and survive the smell of unbathed bodies. When we'd ask, she usually shrugged off the question by saying she was so engrossed in the conversation she hardly noticed the smell. I couldn't understand that…until God called me into a public ministry.

People now sometimes ask me how, after singing for an hour and a half, I can stand and hold a weeping woman as she tells me of the loss of her child. I've often wondered how I can sing softly almost all night by the bedside of a friend in pain and not grow tired until the sun comes up and the medication does its job. Must be in the genes. How does that work, anyway?

I recently heard a traveler to Africa tell this story, which in many ways illustrated what my mother did: "Standing in a large clearing, I watched as a group of elephants approached a deep creek. As is often the case with our children, the young ones went on ahead of the adults and reached the river first. The baby elephants made their way into the water. I stood by, helplessly watching as the water was much too deep for them. It swirled around them and they began to sink and would surely drown.

"Then, much to my delight and amazement, the larger elephants moved several yards upstream and began to lay their massive bodies down into the river. They actually created a dam effect by stopping the raging waters for several minutes. It was enough time to allow the young ones to gain enough footing so they could stand and cross to safety."

When Mom reached out to her neighbors and to those in need in our small town, she didn't have a Bible degree, a pulpit, or a microphone. She did have some quarts of blueberries and an empty passenger seat with a full tank of love from Jesus. And she was, in her own way, showing a willingness to lie down in the water so someone else could gain their footing and cross to safety.

Christine Wyrtzen is a musician, author, seminar speaker, and radio host of the nationally syndicated programs, *A Touch of Encouragement* and *A Gift of Encouragement*. Her most recent book, *Carry Me*, is published by Moody Press. Christine's mother, Gertrude Hewitt, is a homemaker in Petersburg, New York. Mrs. Hewitt enjoys gardening, baking, hiking for blueberries, and quilt-making.

CHAPTER TWENTY-THREE

TCHAIKOVSKY'S 1812 OVERTURE AND CORN ON THE COB

by Jaime S. Wyrtzen

Dinner time is always interesting at our house. My mother is not particularly gifted in the area of jokes. My dad sits at the end of the table, rolling his eyes as he watches my brother Ryan and me crack up over Mom's inability to get the punch line of a joke someone has just told.

Mom's sense of humor is a little different. For example, one night as we were eating dinner, Mom put *Tchaikovsky's 1812 Overture* on the stereo. We were eating our corn on the cob as the drums and cannons boomed. Our mouths were crunching down on the ears of corn in rhythm to the music until Dad finally said, "Christine, this isn't exactly dinner music. I've got indigestion and my jaw hurts from keeping time with the music."

Mom laughed until she cried.

Mom has made growing up entertaining for my brother and me. She always gets involved with playtime. She made up a game for us to play when we rode in the car. She would make up the line of a song, sing it, then I'd come up with a second line that rhymed and so on around the family. Mozart would roll over in his coffin at our creations!

Mom can be tough when she needs to be, but she also knows when to soften and cuddle. When I've had a hard day at school, I know I always have warm arms to come home to. Mom often gets out my own china teacup, pours my favorite tea, sits down, and listens attentively. She always encourages me to talk about my feelings. In fact, from my mother, I have learned how to deal with hard times. Her greatest gift to me is probably the lesson on how to handle pain.

Whenever negative feelings surface in my life, Mom and I sit down and discuss what's going on inside. We try to get to the root of the problem. Then we pray together and Mom encourages me to do something I enjoy—listening to music, writing, taking a walk. She is always quick to remind me that I can do something positive with pain, that many of the world's most talented people drew upon their pain and produced some of history's most wonderful pieces of art, literature, and music. My mom always says, "Transforming pain into something productive changes it from a negative to a bittersweet."

My mother uses her music and journaling to work through rough points in her life. I began to catch onto this when I was around ten. At this time of my life, I was not only dealing with the normal preteen issues, but with the issue of being adopted. I was adopted as a three-day-old infant and I knew almost nothing about my background, so I was angry and had certain fears.

Mom encouraged me to face my fears and anger by talking about it and by keeping a journal. After a while of writing, the emotions that had built up inside me began to find release. Not only did journaling help me work through my feelings, but through it I found out that I love to write. I'm now thinking about pursuing a writing major in college.

I have watched my mom as she relates to people through her music. She is always reaching out to people, not only through her music but through her compassion—always giving a sympathetic hug to someone in need. I have seen her eyes fill up with tears over someone else's pain. She has taught me how to care about people and she has helped me learn to let down my guard so that I can be vulnerable and love others.

As I look back over my seventeen years, I realize how much God has used my mother to help me grow to be a stronger person. Now that I have reached the other side of certain mountains I faced, I am less afraid of the future. I remember, "Greater is He that is in me than He that is in the world" (1 John 4:4). Could a mother teach her daughter any more valuable a lesson than this? I don't think so.

Jaime S. Wyrtzen is a seventeen-year-old college student who enjoys antique and flea markets, bookstores, and gourmet cooking. Her mother is Christine Wyrtzen, creator of Chapel of the Air's *Critter County*, speaker, singer, and author.

CHAPTER TWENTY-FOUR

IF I HAD A NICKEL
by Neva Coyle

*H*igh on the top of a mountain in California's Mojave Desert, Mom held my hand as we walked from Grandma's cabin to our own rough, someday-to-be-finished house. It was my favorite time. It was when Mom and I sang together.

"If I had a nickel..." Mom's sweet voice carried through the open air and played upon the breeze whistling through the screened windows of the chicken house. "...You know what I would do? I'd spend it all on candy and give it all to you! 'Cause that's how much I love you honey..." She'd smile at me and I knew she loved me much more than just a nickel's worth of candy. No matter what, I had my Mom's entire heart.

Mom always had time for me. "My baby girl," she'd say with affection. There were five children in all—three girls, two boys. I lined up in the very middle—the youngest daughter with two little brothers. But I was always Mom's "favorite baby girl." Each of us was her favorite something.

I took my mother's many gifts for granted. Her poetry and short stories came as natural as doing laundry in the wringer washer, feeding her thousand or more chickens, and making chocolate chip cookies. Mom handled a hammer and her rolling pin with equal ease and ability. I wasn't amazed at her talent for sculpture, playing the piano, or "dressing" a chicken for Sunday dinner. I didn't wonder that she took care of Grandma, confined to her bed with tuberculosis, or gladly took her turn at bathing old Mrs. Dye down in the valley, not much more than a vegetable after a stroke.

It didn't surprise me that she and Dad held Sunday school at home or that she gave her piano to the new little Free Methodist Church in town. And, when Mom decided to learn oil painting, why not? Was there anything Mom couldn't do? After all, she could sew, bake, make beautiful paper dolls out of the cardboard from her writing tablet, and craft doll cradles from oatmeal boxes. She could grow anything in almost any climate and in any kind of dirt.

Growing up around such a remarkable role model made trying new things, exploring different options, and finding creative alternatives seem like normal life. She encouraged us to use our imaginations while keeping in touch with reality. She expected her daughters to be feminine without being helpless, to be resourceful without being demanding. She kept our home full of love, joy, and optimism.

Only in reflection have I come to realize how hard Mom's life has been, how little she and Dad had financially, and what difficult challenges she really faced. It's only as an adult, remembering a little five-foot woman carrying a load that would tire a brawny man, that I understand how industrious she was.

But, the most remarkable thing about my Mom has been, and still is, her faith—her unwavering faith-born ability to see beyond any circumstance and make the best of it, even the most difficult situations. She loves God and knows him intimately. She knows the power of prayer and keeps believing in God's touch and intervention for her family, even though we're all in our forties and fifties now. And all through my growing up years she instilled that same faith in me.

How has she influenced my life? I can't think of one single way she *hasn't*. Many times I've said thank you. I'm grateful for the opportunity to say it again.

Thanks, Mom. Thanks for being simple, loving, remarkable, irreplaceable you.

Neva Coyle author of more than thirty books, both non-fiction and fiction, is married to Lee; together they have raised three children. Neva is active in her local church in prayer and women's ministries. She and her husband make their home in California. May Frances Stephenson is Neva's mother. Over the past years she has been involved in many ministries, including serving as Missionary Chairperson and Vacation Bible School Director, and being involved in women's ministries. She is an avid reader, loves to write and paint, and has even taught herself to draw house plans and blue prints!

CHAPTER TWENTY-FIVE

BROWN HANDS AND FEET OF CLAY:
LESSONS I LEARNED IN MOTHER'S GARDEN
by Liz Curtis Higgs

*M*y mother was an award-winning gardener. I, on the other hand, can't keep one green plant alive longer than thirty days.

And that about sums up our mother-daughter relationship.

Mom was almost forty-three when I was born. I was a surprise. A shock. A disaster, even. She'd already mothered five children, one right after another. Then, after enjoying nine long years of peace from pregnancy, it was back to maternity clothes for Mother. She was mortified. None of her Garden Club friends were having babies in their forties, for heaven's sake!

We came home from the hospital together in mid-July of 1954. Mom had a pony-sized pill on her hands from day one. Demanding, opinionated, a real pain in the posterior—that was her youngest daughter. Any hope of seizing back her personal life, of having time to pursue her own dreams or make use of her mathematics degree, disappeared between the cloth diapers and powdered formula. No wonder she was angry. No wonder she never said so.

No wonder that during my teenage years when I swooned over boys, my mother solemnly cautioned me, "Marriage and children are not your only option. Do something important with your life." You and I know that what she was doing—raising six children—was the most important job anyone, man or woman, could ever hope to have. But mothering in the fifties went unnoticed. There was no name for what my mother did. In the nineties we'd call her a "stay-at-home" mom, an honorable choice, but she saw herself as "justa" mother.

I close my eyes now—eyes that have experienced life with a new-born firsthand, eyes that have looked upon a high chair dripping with applesauce or much worse—and I understand. I especially understand why my mother's flower garden came to mean more to her than anything or anyone else in her life. It wasn't that she didn't love her family. To the best of her ability, she did. But we could never give her what her garden gave her in colorful, silent abundance: peace. And quiet.

One starlit summer night I called and called out the back door looking for her. "Mom! M-m-o-o-o-m-m-m-m!" No sound, no movement. Had she stumbled in the asparagus patch? Was she lost among the sunflowers? Finally I got a flashlight and bravely ventured out into the spooky garden filled with shadows that didn't resemble my mother at all. After several frantic minutes of searching, I discovered her on the far edge of our property, precariously balanced on a steep embankment, planting marigolds by the light of the moon.

This was the first lesson I learned from my mother: Children notice when you are hiding from them. Even at that young age, I realized that her need to escape from the noise and the nuisance drove Mom to her garden with increasing frequency. Rather than interrupt her, I simply sat in the house and missed her company.

So it is that when my daughter, Lillian, now seven, wanders into my home office and announces to me in a pouty little voice, "Mama, you love writing more than you love me," I snap my laptop computer shut with a decisive click.

"No, I do not!" I assure her, gathering her up in my arms and draping her long legs over mine. "I love you and Matthew and Daddy more than anything else in the world. I enjoy writing very much, but I *love* you!" My mother could not have said this, but I can. Mom taught me that actions speak louder than words, but words help, too.

Of course, I was very proud of my mother's gifts and talents. She could take three flowers, or five or seven (the pros always use an odd number of stems) and create a floral design that captured blue ribbons and filled our house with beauty. Our corner lot was covered with garden beds—along the fences and all around the house, with a big kidney-shaped plot in the backyard. I was not the only one to notice her abilities; gardening gurus from far and wide came to our Front Street house to gawk at my mother's handiwork, which swelled my young heart with pride.

Mom had true gardener's hands—which is to say not green but *brown.* I can still picture her leaning over the kitchen sink, running icy water over her wrists to cool down (try it—it works) and scrubbing her hands with lemon halves to bleach out the stains (this doesn't work at all). More than once while dressing for Bridge Club, she was forced to yank on white cotton gloves, muttering under her breath. Another lesson from Mother: wear gloves in the garden, so you won't have to wear them elsewhere.

Mom may have spent more time with her flowers than she did with me, but at least I always knew where to find her. Arriving home from school each day, I'd find her bent over her poppies or plucking petunias. That round, blue-jeaned bottom pointing skyward was a very comforting sight. Years later, when I visited a garden center displaying a decorative plywood figure of a bent-over woman in polka dot pantaloons, I cried out in astonishment, "That's my mother!"

Except for the pantaloons. Mom's gardening attire consisted of a pair of well-worn work jeans and a man's white dress shirt. Very utilitarian. When she leaned over, the shirt and jeans parted company in the back, leaving an oval of skin exposed to the merciless sun all summer long. By September, she'd develop a chocolate brown tan line the size and shape of a football. Probably no one ever saw it except Dr. Griswold, Daddy and me. Even Mom couldn't see it without a three-way mirror. And who ever spends any time standing in front of one of those?

Certainly not my mother, who thought fashion was just so much vain foolishness. Mom had a very small closet, no bigger than one you might find in a hallway, meant for three coats and an umbrella. Even so, it held all her clothes and some of mine. She had one ensemble that sufficed any time a dress was called for: a white cotton shirt waist with a knife pleated full skirt that swirled when she walked, dotted with green and orange circles that resembled sliced olives. For weddings and such, she added a white hat with an orange and green bow and smashing tangerine high heels. It was very Loretta Young.

Yet a third lesson learned from my mother, who grew up during the Depression and understood the value of a hard-earned dollar: One great outfit beats three cheap ones.

On rainy days, she gardened indoors, giving drinks to house plants that grew wherever she put them—dim corners, stairwells, tops of bookshelves. It didn't matter. They grew. In the basement she had an upside down garden. Put aside any visions of colorful blooms in hanging baskets. These were plant carcasses dangling from nails in the beams. At the store they're called "dried flowers" or, if expensive, "everlastings." But I saw how it was done: WHACK! Then she'd plunge the blooms into water laced with glycerin and other nasty ingredients, tie their toes together and swing them from the rafters. A ghastly business, although it produced delicately preserved flowers that lasted for years in her arrangements, rather than mere days in the garden.

If only I could have prolonged my own mother's life so easily. In the early weeks of 1978, the chronic cough that had haunted her for years finally had a name: emphysema. A hospital became her home. I hated the sterile walls and antiseptic smell and cold bed railings that held a woman who was dying right in front of my eyes. Desperate to bring some cheer her way, one day in February I sneaked in a Hershey's chocolate bar, her favorite.

"Will the doctors mind?" I asked with concern.

"They'll never see it!" she assured me, opening the wrapper with all the enthusiasm of a child.

The last day I saw her alive was Mother's Day. Daddy had brought her home from the hospital, determined to let her enjoy her last months, or days, surrounded by the things and people she loved. My sister Sarah, the recipient of Mom's gardening genes, spent a day weeding and sprucing up the one corner of the garden that Mom could see from her bedside window. I ran the vacuum around, wanting to be helpful, and cooked a dreadful dinner of burned hamburger steak and hard green peas. She loved it. She even ate it.

Four days later, Dad and my brother Tom appeared at the door of my apartment. The minute I saw them, dressed in blue suits on a Thursday afternoon, I knew my mother was gone.

I was twenty-three and utterly alone, without a husband, a best friend, or any knowledge of the Lord to comfort me. Four long, pain-filled years went by before I met my heavenly father and found a love even more unconditional than Mom's had been. And that was when a tiny doubt began to gnaw at me. *Did she know the Lord as Savior? Was she in heaven now, or...? Lord, please let me know that she's with you!*

I began to sift through all my childhood memories of our discussions about faith, religion, God, church. Was she a believer? I remembered one offhanded comment about "faith being a wonderful thing to have." But did she have it? Yes, she went to church on and off, but was that for social reasons or spiritual ones? The longer I searched the scriptures and my heart for an answer, the more discouraged I became.

Finally, I consulted my oldest brother Dave who had nineteen more years with her than I did. I held my breath when I asked him, "Do you think Mother was a Christian?"

He responded slowly and with great care. "Mom had feet of clay. She knew that she was imperfect and filled with doubts."

This was not very comforting. I wanted answers and, impatient as ever, I wanted them now. I begged the Lord, *Show me! Give me a sign, give me some hope of seeing my mother again in heaven.*

No signs appeared, no writing on the wall, no still small voice. Just memories of my mother's garden in the cold, dark winter months. Nothing green, nothing growing, no signs of life. But under the ground, seeds that had been planted in faith and watered in love were waiting for the warmth of the sun to beckon them forth.

I do not know in fact, but I know in faith: my mother's mustard seed knowledge of God was enough. Those long wintry months in the hospital gave her the time she needed to seek his warmth and comfort. I am content to leave any doubt in the Lord's hands. That, and everything else.

Liz Curtis Higgs is a speaker and writer, humorist and encourager. She is the author of six books, including *Only Angels Can Wing It*, as well as a contributing editor to *Today's Christian Woman Magazine*. Liz is married and has two children—Matthew is nine and Lillian is seven. Liz's mother, Elizabeth Amidon, was the mother of six children.

CHAPTER TWENTY-SIX

A HEART TOO BIG FOR HER KITCHEN
by Annette LaPlaca

My mother's kitchen drives me crazy. Her counters are cluttered with an array of canisters, a mixer, a toaster, and an electric can opener, plus an enormous microwave that takes up way too much space.

Her refrigerator is plastered with photographs—mostly of the eight grandchildren—and phone messages, all of them secured by cutsie fridge magnets that were presents from her second and third grade students.

Since their house is the central meeting place for my siblings who live nearby, the kitchen becomes a combination storage warehouse/mail-call office. My sister drops off her daughter's hand-me-downs so that my sister-in-law can pick them up the next time she comes by. Mail for my younger brother stacks up. He's single and moves around a lot, but you can always send a birthday card or a book to Mom's and he will get it eventually. A pile of books is collecting—donations for my older brother's used book business.

The back door of the house opens into the kitchen. The entry way is crowded with garbage and recycling ready to be sorted in the garage, a rack with everybody's car keys (not house keys—the house is rarely locked), a noisy cuckoo clock, a pile of muddy boots, or shoes—and sometimes socks—and my little sister's puppy, Shadow, waiting to go out.

And on top of all that clutter, Mom cooks for and cleans up after a virtually continuous flow of family and friends.

Whew!

But that's Mom. Her heart is too big for her kitchen. When it comes to caring for people, there is always room for one more.

And the people keep coming. That doesn't surprise me, because I know what draws them: my mom lives the love of Christ in a sad and troubled world. She's exactly the kind of person you'd want to bring your pain and problems to because she won't be shocked or put off, and she'll reach out to offer the peace of Christ and the wisdom of Scripture.

Mom loves children and is constantly taking them into her life and love. She had four natural children and two adopted (I'm biological offspring number two). Over the years she's taken in stray nieces and numerous long-term foster kids. My adopted sister Dawn came from Korea after we'd sponsored her for a few years. Later, Mom felt a special burden for the Hmong students, the children of Laotian refugees, whom she taught in public school. She developed a correspondence course with them—creating lesson materials and supplying incentive awards for them. When I was a child, we had a weekly neighborhood Bible club in our home and our friends always felt welcome at our house—to the point where they helped themselves to pretzels and Doritos right out of our kitchen cabinets.

The county wouldn't let Mom have foster kids when I was young. State law decreed that she already had enough kids in her house. But as soon as most of us were grown, she and Dad were taking in abused children. Eventually Mom and Dad adopted my youngest sister. She's ten—and they're in their late fifties. Mom currently teaches at a small Christian school, where her class is heavily loaded with students who have special needs. And, lately, my folks have been talking about taking on another foster child. Mom just can't bear the thought of children going unloved and unreached for the kingdom of God.

Mom and I have always gotten along well (yep, even when I was a teenager), and we often enjoy the same books or movies. We both like to hit garage sales and antique malls. But our personalities and talents are very different. I have no aspirations to have six-plus children. I'd make a lousy teacher. And, unlike Mom, I have a good sense of direction and logic. You'd never catch me driving my car around and around the gas station pump, hoping the tank opening would somehow suddenly be on the pump side of the car.

Still, I often find myself striving to be like her, because in many ways that comes awfully close to striving to be like Christ.

I want to be in love with the Lord the way my mother is. I remember when she replaced an old, favorite Bible. It was thick and warped from bathtub steam. (The bathtub was one of the only places Mom could go to be alone with God.) And my memory is imprinted with a familiar picture of her in the semi-dark early morning, on her knees, with her face buried in the couch. Even now, I know, she and my father are praying for me, for my husband, and for our two children. God's word and his Spirit equipped Mom for the challenges of her life.

I want to love my children the way she loved me and my siblings— teaching us how to work, how to play, how to get along with others, how to make our lives on earth meaningful in terms of eternal life. I want others to be drawn to me for the same reasons others are drawn to Mom: because people are hungry for Christ, and there's something nourishing about being with those who love him dearly.

By example, Mom's taught me almost everything I need to know about being a woman of God. Trying to be just like her would probably put me in therapy, but learning from her successes has been one of God's gifts to me.

Meanwhile, my kitchen counters are a mess. Ever since my Mom bought me a microwave, I can't seem to find enough space for baby bottles, an occasional pacifier, the box of animal crackers, too brown bananas, the mail, phone messages, a pair of shoes I want to send to my niece, the warranty for the cordless phone, a friend's Tupperware that needs to be returned, last Sunday's bulletin from church, recipes....

I only hope that, like my mother, my heart will also be too big for my kitchen.

Annette LaPlaca is the mother of a two-year-old and a three-month-old, as well as an associate editor for *Marriage Partnership*. Her most recent book is *The Sunday Morning Fun Book*, published by Harold Shaw Publishers. In 1992 Annette and her mother, Joyce Heinrich, wrote a book together entitled *Making Summer Count*, also published by Harold Shaw. Annette's mother teaches second- and third-graders in a Christian school and enjoys spending time with her six children and eight grandchildren.

CHAPTER TWENTY-SEVEN

LESSON UNINTENDED
by Jeanne Hendricks

*M*y mother was not sophisticated but she seized life with a serious purpose. She never compromised her principles of integrity, and she never complained, nor did she quit when the going was rough. She was solid and sensible.

Mother had no romantic fantasies about herself. She frankly admitted that she was not gifted domestically, although she functioned quite adequately. She knew she was not a raving beauty, but she dressed elegantly and tastefully. She was always looking for new ways to grow—four years of Bible school at night (with time out for another baby), advanced tailoring, basic business, and banking. She visited the library often, taught Sunday school at our church, and learned to drive a car when most women didn't. She often visited art museums or science exhibits.

My mother's loyalty to my father was legendary. When he worked at night, she arranged her schedule so she would be up when he came home. During the Depression, I can remember going with her to take his hot lunch when he had to work long hours without a break. She helped him with car repairs—he was an inveterate do-it-yourself-er. She stayed with him almost constantly when he was hospitalized, and during the long final illness that took his life in his mid-life years my mother nursed him around the clock.

But what is possibly the greatest lesson Mother ever taught me was unintentional. At age fifty-five, she modeled widowhood with a dignity I'd rarely seen.

During Dad's terminal illness she had to spend all of their life savings, with no assets left except her small row house and a tiny family property in Maryland. Two weeks after Dad's funeral, Mother was so physically spent she had to have surgery. Before she went into the hospital, she called each of her daughters to tell us that she was praying that she would not wake up from the anesthesia. She felt she had nothing more to do in life and no resources left. She prayed desperately that God would take her home. Mother had never worked in the business world and to face it at age fifty-five must have felt overwhelming.

But God had other plans for my mother. Before she entered the hospital she had timidly applied for a sales position. She pulled through the surgery and when she came out of the anesthesia, she learned that she had been hired by the company and all the paperwork was complete, including a functioning insurance policy. The insurance policy paid all of her medical expenses!

In a short while Mother discovered she was unsuited for sales work and decided to take a banking course. When she filled in the application, she noticed the small print at the bottom of the page, informing her that any student who earned a grade of A would be eligible for tuition refund. My mother got the A and all her money was returned!

Mother's work as a bank teller brought her into contact with a stock broker who encouraged her to let him invest for her. At first, Mother protested that she did not make enough money for investments, but she agreed to consider it. After praying about it, reading, and talking to trusted friends, she took the risk and began investing. At the time of her retirement she did indeed have a sizable nest egg.

Under the sponsorship of her church, Mother went to Mexico for a year to fill in for a missionary-secretary who needed a year furlough. She visited Indian villages on her day off and taught Bible stories with flannel-graph pictures. Later she was able to fulfill a lifelong dream— to visit the Holy Land. It was probably the highlight of all her years. Returning home, she sold her city house, remodeled her little cottage in Maryland, and became involved in the rural community. Soon, various women's groups invited her to show her pictures from Israel. From one country church to another, she told about her trip, always including the gospel message of Christ's love. To her amazement, she saw a number of women trust Christ through her talks.

As the aging process began to steal my mother's alertness, she faced her decline with realism. After hitting a stop sign with her car, she knew that she should not be driving, and she voluntarily surrendered her license.

During the last months of her life, Mother came to our home in Texas to escape the frigid weather of Maryland. Although she was in a wheelchair when she arrived, she determined to exercise her way back to health. Soon she was walking a mile every day. It was during those final months that our friendship deepened. We spent hours reminiscing and talking about her favorite subject, the Lord Jesus. She insisted that I continue traveling with my husband as I had always done. It was during one of those trips that the Lord quickly and quietly called Mother home to himself. I will never stop missing her, but never will I cease to thank God for the gift of a mother who taught me by her example how to live in all kinds of weather.

Someone has said that a mother is not a person to lean on, but someone who makes leaning unnecessary. My mother did that for me.

Jeanne Hendricks' Women of Honor, published by Multnomah Books, is her most recent book. She is an author and speaker who travels worldwide. She and her husband, Howard Hendricks, live in Dallas, Texas. Her mother, Edna Louisa Robertson Wolfe, was a homemaker and bank teller who enjoyed gardening, cooking, and Bible study with her daughter.

CHAPTER TWENTY-EIGHT

LITTLE THINGS, IMPORTANT THINGS
by Neta Thiessen Jackson

I never thought I took after my mother. I was a "Daddy's girl." After all, my dad grew up on a sheep, cattle, and wheat ranch in Montana, and I was the original horse-crazy, animal-loving, farm-girl-at-heart—even though both my parents were school teachers and we lived in the city, a fact I often lamented in melodramatic, adolescent angst.

Dad was the child of immigrants. He grew up in a German-speaking, Mennonite home that blessed me and my siblings with a large family of aunts, uncles, and cousins. Oh, how I loved those big, brawny farmer uncles with their characteristic bald heads and twinkling eyes!

Mom's family, on the other hand, it was said, could be traced clear back to the Mayflower. But that was only a dry statistic to me, missing real flesh-and-blood relatives, since my Mom was orphaned at age thirteen and rarely talked about the tragedy that robbed her of parents and siblings.

I strongly identified with my pull-yourself-up-by-your-bootstraps father. He was definitely the dominant parent, energetic, bustling, busy. He was strict but loving, serious but with a sense of humor that allowed him to laugh at himself. In fact, he was immensely teasable, especially about his bald head. He was also deeply committed to Scripture, the Christian life, and Christian education. If he felt something was wrong or needed to be done, he spoke up, whether it was home, school or church. He was always writing letters to the editor. He was a man of deep conviction, and I admired him deeply.

In the meantime, my Mom was quietly present in the background supporting my dad, reading her books, knowing things, raising her flowers, teaching French or Latin, or organizing the school library as needed, always with a good word to say about everyone, and never wanting to make waves.

My mother was slow and steady; I "bounced." My mother was content to let others forge the way; I plowed ahead, often with more enthusiasm than wisdom.

I was definitely not a "background" person.

So when did I begin to realize that I am more like my mother than I ever imagined? So much so that many old friends who knew my parents often say to me, "You are so like your mother!" At first it was a shock to hear that, but now I am deeply thankful to own the gifts my mother has given me.

First of all, my mother gave me a love of reading. She was a librarian by vocation, and she lived among books every day. Books donated to the school library would show up on my bed, an invitation to be read first before being "catalogued and shelved." Birthdays and Christmas always brought forth new books—wonderful classics like the Laura Ingalls Wilder books, the Children's Bookhouse, and all the horse books by Marguerite Henry, as well as Greek myths and fairy tales and animal stories like *Beautiful Joe*, *Sounder*, *Old Yeller*, and *Black Beauty*.

Later in her life, my mother frequently complained that she didn't have time to read—but we often caught her leaning against a doorway for an hour at a time with a book which she had started in the middle because she was only going to read "for a few minutes."

But it wasn't just a love of reading that energized my mother. It was love of learning. She was interested in everything. And she made it very clear that a good education was not knowing everything, but knowing where to find the information you wanted to know. If someone, whether a student or a family member, asked her a question she didn't know the answer to, she didn't rest until she had discovered the answer. As my own children were growing up, they picked up on this amazing trait, and "ask Grandma" became the byword whenever anyone had a question about anything. And sure enough, whether it took a day or a week or a month, one day that phone would ring and there would be Grandma's answer.

I have to smile at myself even now as dinner conversations are regularly interrupted while I run for the dictionary, encyclopedia or whatever resource is best because someone has asked a tantalizing question.

My mother couldn't understand people who were bored. "I've never been bored a minute of my life," she'd say in amazement. Her list of projects was always longer than the minutes in a day—potting plants, putting together photo albums, sewing doll clothes, writing letters....

Always letters. My mother kept alive the nearly extinct art of correspondence. She and my father moved to different states several times in their fifty-plus years of married life, and she kept up with old friends who went way back. A childhood friend of mine recently said to me, "The death of your mother really hit me when my birthday came around and there was no birthday note from your mother. No matter where I was around the world, your mother's birthday note would always find me." Toward the end of her life, keeping up with her correspondence became my mother's daily "work."

I see my mother in myself in my list of projects—longer than the minutes in a day—and the fact that I love to write letters. Long letters. Thanks to Mom, I can also say I'm *rarely* bored (can't honestly say "never"). Why, even standing in lines is an opportunity to read that book I have tucked into my bag or write a quick note to that childhood friend.

My mother also seemed to notice (and remember!) the "little things." This became even more apparent to me after I was grown and had my own home. If my kitchen drawer lacked a good paring knife, it would show up at Christmas. If I happened to mention that I really love cantaloupe with ice cream, guess what I got for dessert the next time we visited? Gifts almost always "hit the nail on the head" for adults and children because Mom had her antennae out. Expensive gifts? Never. Thoughtful gifts? Always.

Looking back, I can see my mother taught me early to appreciate the "little things" in life. As valedictorian of my high school class, I had the opportunity to give my classmates a "here we go into the future" speech. My topic? "Don't get too busy or too self-important to appreciate the little things in life." In college, when friends were going through hard times, I would send them little notes I called "uplifts" to be opened at a certain day and hour: cartoons, jokes, riddles, quotable quotes, Scripture. Little things. Important things.

My mother could never be accused of being a "home decorator," but her house and yard were always full of blooming plants. Everyone said my mother had a green thumb. Strange, as a girl I was never that interested. I never learned anything about plants from her. They were just "Mom's plants." I'm not sure when it happened, but if you walked into my house today, you would see that even after ten years in our present house, none of the windows have curtains—but every window has a hanging plant, lush greenery everywhere. Ignorant and "all thumbs," I nonetheless plug away every spring on my outdoor flower garden. I wish more of my mother's plant knowledge had rubbed off on me, but one thing I've discovered is it's the digging in the dirt that counts. It renews. It heals.

Mom must have known that. She suffered several terrible tragedies in her life. Her parents and siblings were killed in a tornado. Her car hit and killed a little girl that dashed out into the street. My father died in a car accident. Terrible sorrow, hidden deep beneath her quiet ways. But she was never moody, morose or bitter. She continued to take delight in the little things of life: cups of tea shared, a letter from a friend, potting plants.

When my mother died three years ago, I got up early every morning and planted flowers. It was the most healing thing I could have done. It was so...basic. So in touch with life.

Just the other day, worn out from wrestling with the big issues of church and society like racism, politics, leadership struggles, programs, moral issues, on and on—my father in me—I said to a friend, "When all is said and done, there are three basic things in life that are renewing and healing: babies, pets and gardening." And we laughed in mutual understanding. When life gets tense, both of us find peace and joy in enjoying our grandchildren, walking the dog or pulling weeds in the garden.

That's you, Mom. You in me. You always knew what was important, basic. You softened the corners of my life. You modeled the "home" to come home to. You gave me the foundations to build on—the ways to keep in touch with family, friends, God, the creation.

The little things.
The important things.
The things that count.

Neta Thiessen Jackson is co-author, with husband David, of the *Trailblazer Series*, a line of historical fiction about great Christian heroes and heroines of the faith for young people. Neta has two married children and a Cambodian foster daughter, and she has recently become a grandmother. Neta's mother, Margaret Richards Thiessen, was a Christian school librarian in Seattle, Washington.

CHAPTER TWENTY-NINE

MOM, YOU'RE INCREDIBLE
by Linda Weber

A lot is expected of moms today. I want to say things were better for my mother. I suppose they were in a way. Being a mom was considered a full-time effort back then. No one chided, "You don't belong at home. Get out in the world and make a difference." She was never challenged to opt for a different focus or to build a career. In her generation, if you were a mom, that's just who you were, first and foremost. Anything else was extra—and secondary.

On the other hand, things were a lot harder for Mom. She had three children to raise and an angry, abusive husband to contend with until he finally abandoned us. The responsibility of providing for the family always fell on her shoulders. If we were going to eat, she had to work. And back then, the job market for women was limited, both in choices and in pay. As I recall, she never made more than $200 a month.

We lived in an apple orchard in a small structure built to house migrant workers. A couch sat against one wall of our tiny living room, and an old upright piano covered the opposite wall. If I stood in the center of the room, I could reach out and touch both pieces at the same time.

Cold floors. No carpet. An oil stove for heat. The rent was $25 a month. We used spare apple boxes for cupboards and dressers and covered them with old tea towels. We were allowed to collect the fallen apples, and we added to them the wild asparagus that grew here and there among the trees.

When the school year began, if we kids were lucky, we'd get to choose one pair of shoes to last us the year. Naturally, our wardrobe selection left more than a little to be desired. Most of our clothes were hand-me-downs from other families. Occasionally, our grandmother would buy Easter dresses for my sister and me. When I got into high school, a friend's mom made clothes for me so I could look like everyone else.

What Mom lacked in wealth, however, she made up for in character. She was a devout woman with a steady, thankful heart. She loved her God and read the Bible morning and night. She lived what she learned and never did anything she feared was wrong—not even reusing a postage stamp that had been missed by the cancellation stamp. She trusted that God could handle anything we had to face, and she told us time and again, "God knows our need. He loves us. He'll provide."

For all her sacrifices, for all she did without, Mom never made us feel it was our fault or that she was missing out on something. She never gave the impression she was "stuck" raising the three of us. She never gave those impressions because she never felt that way.

Mom was giving her all to one thing—mothering. Working was a necessary part of that, but her priorities were never confused. She couldn't provide all the things we thought we needed. She couldn't sit back and enjoy much leisure. But she could do one thing as well as anyone, regardless of resources or status: She could be a full-time, all-out mom. She could invest her life in her children. And that she did with passion.

We got by. Mom kept a positive attitude while she focused on the heart and spirit. She understood the importance of giving her best efforts to what was most important—her children. Though Mom didn't give us a high standard of living, she gave us a high standard of life. It didn't matter how many rooms our little migrant house had—what mattered was what went on in those rooms.

Linda Weber is a conference speaker and the author of the best-selling book, *Mom, You're Incredible.* She is married to Stu, a pastor, conference speaker, and best-selling author, and they have raised three sons. Both Linda and Stu are national speakers for FamilyLife conferences. Making and recording family memories has always been Linda's specialty. Her mother, June Lininger, lives in Tyler, Texas, and enjoys reaching out to people who need encouragement.

Condensed from chapter 1 of *Mom, You're Incredible* by Linda Weber. Published by Focus on the Family, 1994.

CHAPTER THIRTY

I WILL NEVER MAKE MY CHILDREN
EAT SPINACH
by Crystal Kirgiss

There once was a time when I whispered under my breath, "I will never, never, never, be like my mother. I will not make my children help with the cleaning. I will not make them fold the laundry. I will not make them wear ugly glasses. Most especially, I will not make them eat spinach."

Of course, I didn't dare speak my discontent. Mother, you see, was not someone to be trifled with. Mother took no guff. Mother was, so far as I knew, immediately below God on the spiritual ladder. So to think of ever speaking such blasphemy out loud was beyond my imagination. Instead, I contented myself with imagining it all in my mind, dreaming about how wonderful it would undoubtedly feel to someday say, "No ma'am, I am definitely not eating that ugly smelling stuff for dinner."

When I was young, you see, I was very silly.

The winter I was seven, I desperately wanted a very certain something for Christmas. I knew that, were I not to receive it, I would simply die. So I dropped hints left and right to my parents. I begged and pleaded and made promises too big for any seven-year-old to keep. And I envisioned a thousand times in my head the perfect Christmas morning when I would unwrap and savor "it"—that certain something.

Today, I do not remember what "it" was, exactly. But by golly, when I was seven, "it" meant the world to me.

Sometime in the middle of December, I realized I was not going to find "it" under the tree on Christmas morning. My mother's evasive responses, her subtle way of changing the subject whenever "it" came up, her comments about how unimportant "it" really was—they all added up to only one thing. The worst Christmas of my life.

And this is when I started to mutter under my breath.

"I will never, never, never be so mean when I'm a mother. I will buy anything my children want!"

Oh, I was angry. Seething. Irate. Positively enraged. Why did *everyone* else get *whatever* they wanted? Why did we *always* have to count our pennies and go without? Why did I have parents who *never* bought me what I wanted?

I lost all hope for living a worthwhile life. Without "it," I may just as well shrivel up and die. I may just as well find a lake and jump in. I may just as well resign myself to a meaningless existence.

All at the age of seven, mind you.

While I pouted and sulked and let my eyes and mouth droop so low that my mother said, "Soon your face will get stuck and look like that forever," I did a terrible thing. I doubted my mother's love for me. Such silly creatures are children that they periodically measure their parent's affection by such meaningless gauges as "it."

But on Christmas morning, my muttering stopped.

For when I opened the gift from my mother, I stared down at a handmade doll of such beauty I was stunned. She boasted hand-stitched eyes, curls of golden yarn, felt button shoes, white eyelet pan-taloons, a violet gingham dress, sheer billowy apron, and a dainty bon-net balanced on the back of her head. And she stared back at me as if to say, "You silly, silly girl."

I glanced at my mother, who was sitting quietly, expectantly, and I saw the reserved excitement in her eyes. I felt ashamed as I imagined the late hours she must have spent each evening carefully choosing fab-ric, tenderly crafting a body, artistically creating a face as she spun love into a small and dainty muslin form.

What ridiculous thing had I done in doubting my mother's love for me?

As I sat in our small, cozy living room, I bent my head, picked up my Christmas child, and whispered, "She's perfect."

At seven, my mother taught me that giving is better than receiving, that pouring oneself into a gift is a form of grace, that "it" cannot possibly hold a candle to a mother's love.

My mother grew up on a farm in Nebraska.

So in addition to tolerating no critical words about the Midwest prairies, her heritage deemed that my mother could not and would not tolerate wasteful living on any level.

With this in mind, the reality of life was this: we were allowed to use no more than three squares of toilet paper at any one sitting.

Woe to those who squandered the toilet paper, or anything else. String was reused. Wrapping paper was smoothed and re-folded. Bread bag twist ties were straightened and saved. Everything, it seemed, had at least two or three lives and as many different uses. And all those precious things were stored in one of two places: the junk drawer or piles. Piles on the desk. Piles under the beds. Piles in the garage.

Piles were the stuff of life.

Besides living and breathing thrift, my mother had the stick-to-it-ive-ness that can only be attributed to her homesteading prairie ancestors. What one began, one finished.

Piano lessons, for instance.

For years, I bemoaned the existence of the eighty-eight-keyed monster in the living room. Yes, yes, I liked to play it. In fact, I loved to play it. I could spend endless hours pounding away at the notes and bellowing at the top of my lungs.

I just didn't want to *study* it, thank you.

"Sorry," said my mother. "You started. You will finish."

Finishing meant: you will take lessons until you no longer live under my roof.

At which point I promptly left for college and majored in piano performance.

My mother's parents were never very happy about the fact that my father took their daughter and their grandchildren far from the Nebraska farm to live in the noisy and crowded suburbs of Chicago.

My mother resolved to make up for this as best she could.

Mostly, this meant packing us up as often as possible and bundling us off to the far away plains. When I was smaller, we traveled by train, the mighty Zephyr that left Chicago's Union Station in the afternoon and arrived in Holdredge, Nebraska, in the middle of the night. We climbed aboard the powerful and mysterious silver giant and crossed our fingers that we would get seats next to the water fountain with its neat stack of cone-shaped paper cups.

All I remember of those trips is the click-clack of the rails, the frightening way the alcoves between the cars jiggled and jolted and roared when one tried to walk the entire length of the train, and the white-linen elegance of the dining car, a place where one was allowed to eat only if one was very well behaved, very rich, and very lucky. We, alas, were not very rich according to Mother, so we ate lunch brought from home.

As I grew older, the trip was made by automobile countless times, usually with a maniac feline who was headed for a better life in the country, and once or twice in a little single engine plane. Either way, I threw up, a dramatic and trying affair that left my mother looking weary.

However we managed to get there, a trip to the farm was reassuring. We'd drive to old family homesteads, to ancient houses standing empty in the middle of the prairie, to cemeteries where three generations of relatives lay and to the sites of long-gone schools and churches. We'd explore the old two-room home in which my mother lived as a child, dress up in old clothes stored in the attic, and listen to stories of what life used to be like when schools were always ten miles from home, and the walk, both ways, was uphill. We'd soak in the sounds of doves and crickets, marvel at the distance one could see in any given direction and grow heady with the scents of the land and the vegetation it produced.

My mother linked me to her heritage during these trips, and I slowly realized I was part of something much bigger than myself—I was a part of history. I felt as though I belonged and I mattered and I had a place.

For a child, few things are more comforting.

After my marriage, God, in His infinitely humorous wisdom, saw fit to give me three sons at near-perfect two year intervals. This meant that for a period of four years I felt as though I had no life.

During this time, I came to an abrupt and startling appreciation of my mother.

Certainly I'd not tested her patience nor sapped her sanity to the same extent as my own children, had I? Nor could I believe that I'd ever complained so much about the dinner menu, or household chores, or piano practice.

And where, I wondered, did this incessant urge come from to create things, to pour myself into a gift? And for goodness sake, why was I saving all these Styrofoam meat trays and used shoelaces? And yes, I know my parent's home is 700 miles away and we were just there three months ago, but wouldn't another visit be wonderful?

There is no doubt. I am my mother's child. When God knit me in her womb, he wisely included much of her pattern in mine. And because he knew, even then, every word I would speak, he heard me muttering at the age of seven "I will never, never, never be like my mother."

And I suppose he laughed.

Crystal Kirgiss is a free-lance writer who is a regular contributor to *Campus Life Magazine*, as well as an award-winning newspaper columnist. Based in Detroit Lakes, Minnesota, Crystal and her husband work with youth in the area as part of the Young Life organization. Crystal's mother, Sara Jacobsen, currently resides in Palentine, Illinois, where she is a teacher's aide in the Mildly Mentally Impaired department of Wheeling High School. Mrs. Jacobsen is also involved in the women's and music ministries of her church.

CHAPTER THIRTY-ONE

ELIZABETH'S UNDER-THE-BED COOKIES
by Diane Noble

My mother, Elizabeth Hill, is a delightful combination of artistry, courage, humor and steadfast love.

For as long as I can remember, Mom has had an artist's heart. At various times in her life she has painted with oils, sculpted with clay, tried her hand at a potter's wheel and even designed and created porcelain dolls.

But as I think back on my growing up years in a small town in the rugged Sierra Nevada mountains, it's my mother's rare eye for beauty—both in nature and life—that I remember. She seemed always to see things with an appreciation—deeper and more intense—than others did.

As we walked along our mountain roads, she would point out the delicate turn of a leaf or the twist of a burnished manzanita branch. Or she might stop, finger to lips, so I would listen to the music of the pines in the wind.

Once she had my father abruptly halt the car as we passed a covey of mountain quail. Almost before the car rolled to a stop, she'd leapt out and scooped up a tiny chick who'd been trailing behind the rest.

With an expression of awe, she held the tiny creature in her palm for me to see. Together we carefully examined its markings and color, its cotton-ball weight, then heaved sighs of relief as Mom released it and the mama quail accepted the chick back into her brood.

I know my love for God's creation is part of the heritage I received from my mother. In each of my novels, whether historical or contemporary, it's as natural as breathing for me to include those same observations my mother made years ago: the dance of light on a quaking aspen, the bubbling music of a mountain stream, the artist's palette of colors in a Pacific sunset.

My mother has always dealt with hardships with courage and humor. Not only does she look for the positive in any given situation, she has always seemed to find the funny side as well.

When I was ten, my mother asked a friend, our very pregnant pastor's wife, to accompany us as she drove me—in our brand new car— to Girl Scout camp. The remote camp required Mom to navigate the car along a rutted, muddy, dirt road miles from our home. In several places, she even had to ford streams, though none were very deep.

She found the camp, deposited me with duffels and sleeping bag, then turned the car around for the journey home. What she didn't know was that after she'd earlier passed one of the streams, water had been released to relieve the pressure on a nearby dam, causing the water-level of the stream to rise rapidly.

Brave as ever, though, my mother assessed the situation, figuring if she'd made it across the first time, she could surely do it again. So she revved up the engine and plowed into the water, only to feel the car settle deep into the mud.

She quickly helped her pregnant friend wade safely to shore, then found some nearby workers to help with the car's rescue. Several hours later, when she finally reached a telephone, she called to tell my father what had happened.

His first question was, "How's the car?"

To which Mom sweetly replied, "It's fine, dear, except for the limit of trout I caught in the back seat."

Mom's enduring, steadfast and sacrificial love raised a family, saw her through fifty years of marriage, and continues to burn as brightly now as ever.

When I was very young, she was never too busy to cuddle my brother or me on her lap, often reading to us or teaching us nursery rhymes. Some of my earliest memories are of her love for words and stories and books.

Later on, she devoted time and energy to a Bible memory program for the neighborhood children, many of whom weren't allowed to attend church. For years she faithfully taught Sunday school and VBS, specializing in unique crafts she developed without books or instruction. Her impact on the children she taught is still being felt. Those same children, now grown with little ones of their own, have stayed in contact with Mom, thanking her for her godly influence in their lives.

Our door was always open to my friends, no matter how silly, giggly, or rowdy. Lively dinners—set with several extra plates—were commonplace, and sleepless slumber parties endured.

Mom kept a plate of fresh-baked cookies on the counter, a simple gift of love for family and friends alike. One little friend took a cookie home for later and hid it under her bed. After her mother found it while vacuuming and tried a nibble, she called everyone in town to trace its origins. The trail led to my mom who was happy to divulge the recipe. It's still known today as the recipe for Elizabeth's Under-the-Bed Cookies.

In my novella, *Gift of Love,* in the Christmas collection, *A Christmas Joy,* I based my fictitious mountain village, Cedar Creek, on my real hometown and related the miraculous story of how the town's only church came into being.

My father was one of the several men who built the church for the town's "women and children." Though the men did the physical work, it was the quiet faith and fervent prayers of the women, my mother among them, that saw the project through to completion.

Real completion. Because once the church was built, God's Spirit swept through that little town and its people, bringing men, women and children to their knees.

I was seven years old at the time, and I'll never forget the sight of my parents and my brother kneeling at the altar, giving their lives to Christ. Our home changed, and Jesus Christ became its center.

When I was eight, one night at bedtime my mother and I talked about what it meant to give your heart to Jesus. I don't remember her exact words, but whatever she said, it touched my young soul.

I knelt beside my little bunk bed and asked Jesus to come into my life. Of all my memories of my mother, this is the most precious: I can still picture her kneeling beside me, holding my hand, as I entered God's kingdom.

Diane Noble writes historical and contemporary romance under the pen name Amanda MacLean. Her recent novels include the trilogy *Westward, Stonehaven,* and *Everlasting;* the Palisades Premier, *Promise Me the Dawn;* and her newest release, *Kingdom Come.* Her mother, Elizabeth Hill, lives beside Lake Norman just outside Charlotte, North Carolina. Widowed for ten years, her artistry, courage, humor, and love have never faltered. She's active in her community and church. Her latest challenge? She's learning to jet ski at age seventy-eight.

CHAPTER THIRTY-TWO

EYES TO SEE
by Ruth Senter

My mother taught me to see. Not that my eyes didn't open by themselves. They did. And from the very beginning Daddy said my eyes were dark brown, just like all the Hollingers. And my mother said my eyes always had a mischievous twinkle, as though I was already on to the next adventure.

My mother did not have to teach me to focus or how to have 20/20 vision. I was born with that ability. Most of my life, I have had perfectly good vision. Only now in my mid-life have I had to turn to bifocals for help.

Still, as I was growing up, my mother taught me how to see. She was always saying to me, "Oh, look, Ruth Ann...."

"Come look at this sunset," Mother would call from the porch. "Have you ever seen so many shades of pink?"

And I would come sit with her on the front porch swing and together we would count the shades of pink.

Or she would look into the west, ablaze in all its glory and sing in her soft contralto voice, "We'll build a little nest, somewhere in the west, and let the rest of the world go by...."

We were far away in southern Alabama, but with my mother I could almost see a cozy cabin, out there on the western prairies somewhere—a flat, drab, square in the middle of all the flurry of pink sunset.

Whether it was a sunset, a bee on the honeysuckle vine, a hummingbird flying backwards or a line of ants marching in long, solemn file up the hill they'd created for themselves, my mother was always calling me to stop what I was doing and "come look."

My mother often loaded our little red wagon with a thermos of lemonade, peanut butter crackers, a blanket and books—bird books, flower books, tree books. Off we would go to the woods—mother, my four brothers and me, off on some sort of hunt.

Sometimes we were hunting dogwood blossoms, or wood violets, or four-leafed clover. Other times, it was birds we were looking for—bluebirds, orioles, red-winged blackbirds. Sometimes we took our pails and hunted down blueberries, raspberries, acorns, pine cones. Always, we were on the lookout for something that God grew in our woods, or painted in our skies, or sprinkled on our pasture.

It was in my mother's nature to always be looking for and appreciating some good gift from God in the world around her. When she and Daddy were young and "courting," they used to spend spring afternoons walking in the woods, looking for trailing arbutus (a plant that grows along the woodland floors and bears pinkish flowers in early spring). And even today, as she is approaching her eightieth year, she is still training her sights on the world beyond herself. She is still an avid bird-watcher and she loves nothing better than to go for a walk in the early morning hours when the dew is still on the grass, or to drive through the rolling hills surrounding the place she and Daddy live. And even after all these years, she is still saying, "Come look...did you see that? Stop. Let's watch that...."

Mother taught me to see God's fingerprints on the world around me. But even more importantly, she taught me to look for God in the pages of his word. And it seemed to me, even as a child, that every time my mother opened her Bible, she found something new about God. And she would tell her children what she had found.

"Isn't that amazing?" she would say to my brothers and me. "Can't you just see Jesus...?" And then my mother would paint the scenes for us—Jesus reaching out his hand and touching the blind man's eyes, taking the little children on his lap, washing his disciple's dirty feet. Through my mother's vivid description of Scripture, I would see Jesus in ways I'd never seen him before. And I learned to keep looking for him in new ways. Those childhood images my mother created for me are forever fixed in my mind—in my thoughts about the person Jesus is and the God he came to earth to represent. My mother taught theology in pictures. And she was always saying, "Can't you just see God...?"

And the amazing thing was that I could—so clear was the picture she had painted for me.

Not that I always wanted to see. Or always willingly stopped to look. I went through turbulent teenage years when I only had eyes for myself. And still today I can so quickly lose focus—see visions of sugarplums dancing in my head, or find myself gazing wistfully at more of this or more of that—more clothes for my wardrobe, more furniture for my house, more landscaping for my yard.

But when all the sights and sounds of longing are cleared away, I return to the simple gift my mother gave me—the ability to see God's gifts all around me and then quietly sit back, enjoy, and give thanks for what he's given.

It is perhaps my mother's greatest legacy to me.

And I am a more contented person because of it.

Ruth Senter is the author of many books, including *Longing for Love* and *Have We Really Come a Long Way, Baby?* She has served as editor of *Partnership Magazine* as well as Senior Editor of *Campus Life*. Ruth's mother, Gertrude Hollinger, lives in Pennsylvania where her husband serves on the pastoral staff of their church. Ruth and her mother enjoy traveling in England and sipping tea together anywhere.

CHAPTER THIRTY-THREE

WINNIE-THE-POOH AND THE FOUNDATIONS OF LIFE

by Jori Senter Stuart

*I*f I believed in fate, I would say my destiny was chosen from the day I was conceived.

"Mark, there's something I need to tell you."

In my mind's eye I can see him huddled over his pile of text books, preparing a sermon for his seminary hermeneutics class the next day. She is sitting on the couch, her legs tucked up under her with a C. S. Lewis book on her lap.

"Huh," he responds, in his best don't-interrupt-me-I'm-concentrating voice.

"Mark...I think you better put down your pen for a minute. We need to talk."

This catches his attention. With a sigh, he closes his notebook and silently prays he doesn't get chosen to deliver his sermon in class tomorrow.

"Okay, I'm listening." He stretches his long legs out in front of him and crosses them. His attention is on her completely now. "We are, uh, well, uh...." Although it is well rehearsed in her mind, the words just don't come out the way she had planned.

"Ah...well...I just wanted to let you know that...ah...we will need another ticket for graduation in the spring." She looks at him, hoping he will catch the clue.

"Great, is your mom coming?"

"Um, no, it's not my mom. Actually, honey, it will be another *Senter*."

"My dad's coming?"

"Well, no, that's not *exactly* who I was talking about...." She pauses, then decides to cut the subtlety.

"Actually, it will be a baby."

Silence.

"A baby? Our baby?"

Although I was there but not conscious during that conversation, I imagine it may have sounded something like that. I do know that it didn't take long after that conversation took place for my parents to introduce me, *in vitro*, to the finer things of life. Shortly after my mother's not-so-subtle announcement to my father, he came home with a present for her—a present that became a family treasure. It was a gift that has forever shaped who I am. A gift that fostered many hours huddled under the covers during the cold Chicago winters, as Mom read the stories from within this gift. A gift I would later receive as a twenty-five-year-old with a family of my own, in the hopes that someday I would share it with my children as my parents had shared it with me. It was a book of Winnie-the-Pooh—a book he had loved as a child.

Eight months later, as my mother panted and pushed and struggled to give me life, my father (who was in the middle of final exams at the time), read aloud the stories of Christopher Robin, Eeyore, and Tigger. Between contractions he read about Winnie-the-Pooh getting stuck in Rabbit's hole after eating too much honey, and about the time that Piglet met a Heffalump. When I finally did enter the world, at 9:23 P.M. on June 4, 1970, the books of A. A. Milne were not very far away.

I was destined to love books.

As I grew older, my fondest memories include Mom, my brother Nicky and me, crawling into bed together as the cold winds blew through the cracks in the window panes, to travel back through time to a little sod house on the banks of Plum Creek with Laura Ingalls Wilder. It took us several years, but together we read through the entire set of Laura's books chapter by chapter, night by night.

Although Mom didn't know it, during those cozy winter nights she was laying a foundation for me. She was teaching me a fundamental lesson that would impact the rest of my life.

She was teaching me that to read was to live…and to live life to its fullest.

She continued that teaching as I grew older.

When other kids were begging their mothers to take them to the amusement park or the zoo, I was begging my mom to take me to the library. I could ride my bike the two blocks to the library, but since I couldn't carry home the twelve books I wanted to check out (twelve was the maximum number they would allow one to check out per visit), I needed Mom to go with me. And she always did.

By the time I was twelve years old, I had traveled the world with my mother. Together we had been shipwrecked on a desert island with the Swiss Family Robinson, walked with Madeline through Paris in two straight lines, biked to the zoo with the Curious George and the man with the big yellow hat, and walked through the Bible with Maxi and Mini Muffin. We went to Switzerland with a little girl named Heidi and traveled through Canada with Janette Oke. We had even read through the Childcraft books page by page looking for new and exciting projects to work on.

Mom continued to build on the foundation. She stretched me with new books and tougher topics. When I would ask questions she would often respond, "Let's see what we can find out about that," and hand-in-hand we would trot over to the well-used set of World Book Encyclopedia.

And so the next level of the foundation was laid: that books and reading bring wisdom, guidance, and knowledge. And with the power of those three in my hand, I could do almost anything.

Many nights, after we had finished our evening read, Mom would pray with us and kiss us as she tucked the covers underneath our chins. Then she would head off to the typewriter. As an aspiring writer with young children, the only time she had to write was after Nicky and I were tucked safely in bed. The click-click-click of the typewriter keys beat out a rhythm that carried me off to sleep, with the comfort of knowing Mom was not far away.

Mom's writing success was a long time in the making. It came after many nights of my being lulled to sleep by the typewriter. But her writing success did come, and then one day people started asking me, "Are you going to be a writer like your mom when you get older?"

"No way!" I was quick to respond. "Never."

To a teenager, being like Mom is like kissing your brother. The thought was unappealing, to say the least.

I'm sure it hurt my mom to hear me talk like that, but she never showed disappointment. Instead, she would simply bring home the latest Janette Oke title from our Christian bookstore or hand over her well worn copies of *Little Women* and *Christy* to further fan the flame which was already beginning to burn bright within me.

It didn't take long for my negative ideas to change. In college, as I moved away from Mom and Dad, what they did seemed more and more special. Although I still wouldn't admit I wanted to be "just like Mom," my admiration and respect for her grew. All the years of listening to typewriter keys late into the night suddenly had meaning. When my roommate mentioned that one of Mom's books had ministered to her at a time of crisis in her life, my sense of wonder increased—a wonder at how God can use skills that are dedicated to him.

The third level of the foundation was laid.

Books mattered.

They ministered.

They healed.

They changed lives.

I knew then what I was to do with the rest of my life.

These days, I travel thousands of miles and speak to hundreds of people a year about books. I talk to bookstore owners and employees, librarians, parents, and volunteers. I teach, encourage, discuss, argue, and lecture about books. And, of course, I read books. Oh yes, I still read. I average four books a week. More, if I'm lucky.

But all that I have read, all that I believe, and all that I hope to learn is based on one simple but life-changing factor; my mother tirelessly worked from the very beginning to instill in me a love of literature. It is something I will forever be grateful for, and it is something I plan to one day pass along to my children. And I intend to start, as she did, with a story about a wonderful old bear...named Winnie-the-Pooh.

Jori Senter Stuart is a freelance writer and a sales representative for Beacon Distributing, a division of David C. Cook Publishing. Even though Jori lives in Canada and her mom, Ruth Senter, lives in Illinois, the two are still very close. When together, they can be found enjoying each other over coffee and muffins at their favorite breakfast nook or searching local shops for the perfect remembrance of the special trip they took to England. Most often, though, Jori and Ruth can be spotted sitting and discussing their favorite topic—books.

CHAPTER THIRTY-FOUR

NO TEARS FOR HERSELF
by Anne Ortlund

By all outward appearances, my mother would have had plenty of reasons to feel sorry for herself. Her country was in the thick of World War II. Her husband (my father), a U. S. Army general, was in far-off Iran. Her only son, Bobby, an Air Force pilot, had been killed when his plane went down, leaving a wife and three-week-old twins. Her small house was filled to the brim—her three daughters (my two sisters and me) were still living at home, and now her daughter-in-law and new-born twins were moving in.

I was a student at the University of Redlands at the time. When my sister-in-law and her twins moved in, our house was so full I had to sleep on the screened-in porch. I knew my mother had to be grieving deeply over my brother Bobby's death, especially because Daddy was so far away and not there to share it with her. But what I remember most was that my mother didn't fall apart or sit around feeling sorry for herself. She went right on guiding the house and teaching weekly Bible classes the way she'd always done.

In her pain, she didn't focus on her pain. She focused on God. I think that was what made my mother the woman of true "grit" that she was. She didn't dwell on herself.

And my mother raised her children that way too—to focus on God and not on themselves. I saw my mother cry over my sin, but she didn't cry for herself. I often think about this quality in my mother, especially in this day of "meism." My mother didn't live with a "poor-me" attitude.

Mother's name was Betty Sweet, and her name fit her perfectly. She loved to play games with us. She was very competitive and made the games fun. We spent endless hours at Bunko and Chinese Checkers—often with a great deal of noise and hilarity. Army post chapels didn't have Sunday evening services, so every Sunday night was game night. And the family tradition was that Mother always served toasted cheese sandwiches and hot chocolate poured from a Japanese pot that had a broken spout.

Mother made a game out of everything. When she was teaching me the alphabet, we did it by playing games with wooden blocks. One of the first things I remember my mother teaching me was to skip. After that, we were always skipping somewhere together.

The greatest contribution Mother made to my life was probably her zeal and passion for God's word. My parents came to Christ through a Bible study when I was six years old. They were so excited about their new faith that when they got home from the study that night, they woke my brother and me to tell us about the decision they had made to follow Christ. The very next morning, we said grace around the breakfast table for the first time ever.

My mother immediately started studying her Bible. Shortly after their conversion, Daddy was transferred to another Army post. Mother and Daddy looked for a new Bible study to join. When they couldn't find one, they started their own. And for the next forty-some years they taught Bible classes, separately and together. When my mother died at age seventy-nine, she was still teaching weekly Bible classes.

My mother didn't just read God's word in passing—she studied it. For as long as I can remember, Mother got up every morning at 4:30 just to study her Bible and pray. That made a great impression on me, and that impact can be seen in the lives of my own children as well. One of my greatest joys is to study and teach God's word. Our daughter Sherry spends every morning in the corner of a coffee shop so she can be alone and prepare for the Bible classes she teaches. We also have a son who teaches God's word at a seminary, and two sons-in-law in Christian ministry who diligently teach the word. And I'm married to a man who has spent his life preaching the word.

Mother didn't take lightly her responsibility to see that her children walked with God. When I was twelve, we were living in Hawaii where Daddy was stationed. During that time, Donald Barnhouse, a well-known Bible teacher from Philadelphia, was preaching in Honolulu. Mother took me to hear him about ten times, driving fifty miles each round trip. (And that was in the days before super highways.)

One of those nights, on the way home, my mother asked me directly, "Anne, have you given your whole life to God?" That was the night I truly turned myself over to him. From then on, I wanted to serve God the way my mother served him—with my whole heart. And when I became a mother, I sought to pass on to our children that same joy and enthusiasm for serving him.

Another legacy from my mother: she was a vivid example of how to love a husband. Mother and Daddy were true lovers. Daddy died one January. In May of that same year, quite suddenly, Mother had a stroke and died in her sleep. The doctor said, "Your mother didn't want to go on without her roommate!" So she just went quietly and quickly to be with Daddy. We grieved. And we rejoiced. Our parents had lived their lives in the joy of one another's company. Now, four months later, they would just take up where they'd left off.

I am grateful for the woman my mother was. She taught me not only how to remain focused on God in trying times and how to be a husband's best friend, but also how to love God whole-heartedly. It is a legacy, I pray, by God's grace, that I will leave with my own descendants.

Anne Ortlund is the author of fifteen books, including *Disciplines of a Beautiful Woman, Up With Worship* and, her most recent, *In His Presence,* which she co-authored with her husband Ray. She is a much sought after speaker, was for many years a pastor's wife and has raised four children. Currently, she and her husband are involved in a conference and broadcast ministry. Her mother, Betty Sweet, was a Bible teacher for many years, the wife of a career Army general and the mother of four.

CHAPTER THIRTY-FIVE

HOW'D MOTHER GET SO SMART?
by Carol Holquist

There are many things I admire about my mother. Her gifts of compassion and hospitality, her ability to teach. She was a great nurturer—not only of her family (including her siblings, in-laws, cousins, nieces, and nephews), but of her church family and neighborhood friends as well. She raised her four children with a firm hand and an unwavering faith.

But one of the things I admire the most is her godly wisdom. Because of it, she had a fearless and confident approach to life.

I was eighteen years old, a freshman in college with my sights set on an English literature major, riding high with the sense of being on my own for the first time. Then I got back my first English writing assignment. The paper was awash in red ink; the professor's comments were pointed and unsparing. I was devastated. If I couldn't do better than a C on an initial freshman theme assignment, how would I ever manage the rigors of academic life that lay ahead? Feeling like a total failure, I picked up the phone and dialed my mother.

She listened as I sobbed out my story of utter failure. "I guess I'm not capable of doing this. I've never gotten a C in English in my life. Maybe I should just quit now and come home. "This is a waste of my time and your money."

Mother didn't contradict; she responded calmly: "You can come home if you want to. Pack up your things and get ready. I have a few things to finish here, but I'll be there to get you in a couple of hours. If you have everything packed, we can load the car and be back home by supper time."

"Really?" I asked incredulously. Could this be the person who had drummed into our heads that you do not quit, no matter how tough the situation? "Quitters never win and winners never quit." I'd heard it a million times. Had my mother suddenly gone soft?

"Yes," she continued. "Maybe it would be better for you to leave school now before you get even more discouraged. But there is just one thing—I'm not going to tell your dad what's happening. I'll let you explain it to him."

I gulped and felt my knees go weak as I mentally placed myself in front of my Dad. Whatever would I say to this proud father who had worked so hard to send me off to get the opportunity for education he never had? Was I willing to admit to him that my resolve could be blown away by one average mark on a preliminary paper in an introductory course within the first month of school? Suddenly my perspective changed.

"Well, maybe I should stick it out for a few more weeks—you know, see how I do on the next assignment. It would be a shame to leave before I know for sure that this is over my head."

I suddenly found myself voicing the very words I had expected to hear from Mother.

"That's up to you. I'll come get you today if you want me to."

"No," I said slowly. " I think I'd better give it another try."

"Good for you! I was pretty sure you could figure it out for yourself. Now go pull yourself together and get busy on your school work! And don't forget to write Aunt Anne a thank you note for the five dollars she sent you."

Now Mother was sounding like her usual self again.

How did my mother know how to respond to me in that situation? I've wondered about that many times over the thirty-plus years since that memorable day. Dr. James Dobson's counsel was not available for parents in those days. In fact, Mother had probably never even read a parenting book, she didn't put much stock in advice from Ann Landers, and it was not in her personality to discuss parenting issues with anyone outside of perhaps her husband. But what she said to me in those few minutes on the phone that day had tremendous implications for my life.

When I was looking for a way out, she wisely placed the responsibility for my future right where it belonged—on my own shoulders.

I shouldn't have been surprised at my mother's good sense. All my life she had guided me with great wisdom. She was not well educated or even well connected socially. She never bothered to keep up on the latest fashions or trends; few people beyond her family and close circle of friends would recognize her name. But those who knew her would readily acknowledge her wisdom and her ability to teach.

She could always be counted on to slice through all the surface "stuff" and give a quick and no-nonsense "take" on most any situation. She raised her four children with a firm hand, an unwavering faith, and a litany of homespun wisdom. She had an aphorism from Scripture or folk wisdom for nearly every situation: In a tough spot? "Find a way, or make one" or "It's a long road that has no end." Wishing for something unrealistic? "If wishes were horses, beggars could ride." In an ethical dilemma? "Tell the truth and shame the devil." Tempted to take a shortcut? "Haste makes waste" or "Anything worth doing is worth doing well." Procrastinating on an important task? "The road to hell is paved with good intentions." Have some questionable friends? "You are known by the company you keep." Tempted to take compliments too seriously? "Praise is like perfume: it is to be sniffed and enjoyed, but never swallowed." Interestingly enough, I often find myself repeating my mother's words of advice even today.

Her wisdom made a difference in how she looked at pain. By example, Mother taught us to keep a stiff upper lip in the face of adversity but never to take a grim view of life.

I'll never forget the day I cut my hand trying to catch a glass that was falling from the kitchen counter. As she carefully picked the shards of glass from my hand, I winced and said, "Oow—how can you stand to do this when you know how much it hurts!" She paused, gently cradling my bloody, throbbing hand. "I could cut your hand off if I thought it would be good for you," she said calmly. I didn't doubt she was serious.

Mother was accident prone. Some of my earliest memories are of her standing in our kitchen cooking dinner, her hand or fingers cut or burned and wrapped up in gauze. As she grew older she suffered a variety of illnesses and injuries—some unusual and potentially debilitating: she broke a tendon in her thumb, which caused her thumb to "flop"; she fell out of bed during a bad dream; she was diabetic; she suffered three strokes, and as a result, learned to walk again three times after she was eighty years old; she had surgery to clear both carotid arteries; in her later years she suffered from macular degeneration, a particularly bothersome form of blindness that cuts the center out of one's vision; she had a corneal transplant; and she had the expected age-related aches and pains of arthritis.

But until her death, she remained a strong, optimistic, fun-to-have-around person. She never bothered to acknowledge the limitations she faced. She refused to accept defeat at the hands of illness. Mother just kept on going. "It's better to wear out than rust out," she would often say.

Hers has been a sterling example as I've faced chronic pain for much of my own adult life. Except for Mother's showing me the way, I can't imagine how I would have learned the important lesson of not allowing myself or others to define me by my pain.

Mother taught me many things without ever knowing she was instructing. One of the most vital lessons was the importance of choosing a mate wisely.

Dad was a delightful person, and the perfect foil for Mother's practicality. He was clever with his hands (he could repair almost anything); he was loving and possessed a quick wit.

But when Mother met him, he was a diamond in the rough. His childhood was lacking in love, peopled with a parade of stepmothers, and a harsh, demanding father. There was little in his background to commend him as a caring and nurturing husband. But Mother saw his beautiful spirit and tender heart, and that to her was far more important than the right pedigree. Together they built a home where we knew we were secure and cherished above any possession.

One day, one of my sisters threw her arms around Mother and said, "Mommy, you sure did pick us a good Daddy!" She was so right! When it came to choosing my own life partner, Mother's wisdom, years before, had secured for me a solid set of values which would help me choose a man of great integrity and strength.

Mother wasn't perfect: she was a worrier who imparted many of her fears to her children; she could be judgmental and rigid in her beliefs; she was strict beyond reason at times. But even when I may have thought otherwise, she was the perfect mother for me. Not a day goes by that I do not draw from the well of her wisdom and good sense. Her legacy of strength surrounds my thinking and encourages and informs my decisions.

And I am deeply grateful.

Carol Holquist is Associate Publisher for Discovery House Publishers in Grand Rapids, Michigan. She is the mother of two and wife of David, a professor at Calvin College. Her mother, Myrta Bertram Garland, was a mother of four who lived in Cincinatti, Ohio, for more than seventy years.

CHAPTER THIRTY-SIX

LOSING A DREAM, GAINING A FUTURE
by Julie Ackerman Link

The promises made my eyes light up. The places I could go. The people I could meet. The things I could do. I pictured the exotic places. I imagined the fascinating people. I envisioned the exciting opportunities. To a sixteen-year-old girl who had spent her whole life in a small town with the embarrassing name of Fruitport, the enticements offered by the sophisticated young woman seated across the living room were nearly irresistible. I was eager to escape my boring life, and she was offering a ready-made flight plan. It required no thought, no effort, and no entrance exam. Just my mother's signature on a piece of paper.

My mother sat back in her chair and listened patiently as the woman explained the training program, the salary package, and the outstanding benefits. I sat on the edge of my seat, ready to race upstairs, pack my suitcase, and take flight. The friendly skies beckoned as the woman tried to convince me to sign up for a career as a flight attendant.

She didn't have to say much to persuade me. She talked about the type of person they were looking for—friendly, helpful, confident, and outgoing. At sixteen, I was none of those things. I was shy, unsure, emotionally unstable, and introverted. But the traits she mentioned matched the kind of person I wanted to be, so I believed her. Her interest in signing me up made me think that she had made a more accurate assessment of my qualities in thirty minutes than my parents had made in sixteen years.

"I can see that Julie is confident and intelligent," she said. "I'm sure she'll catch on quickly and do very well."

"But what about college?" my mother asked. "Where does that fit in?"

"Oh, she can always go to college," the woman said. "This is a once-in-a-lifetime opportunity. If she's going to do this, she has to do it while she's young." She glanced at me and smiled, assuring me that she was on my side and knew how to handle my mother. "Besides, college is expensive, and this won't cost anything," she said pleasantly. "In fact, Julie will actually earn money while she's being trained."

Money was limited in our family, so I assumed that this information would make my mother's ears perk up. It didn't.

"She may be able to make money for a while," my mom continued, "but there's no future in it. How will it help her later in life?"

"By the time she can no longer work as a flight attendant, she'll be ready to get married and have a family," the woman reasoned. "So there's no need for that to be a major consideration."

When the woman had finished her pitch and had answered my mother's questions, she reached into her leather briefcase and pulled out papers for her to sign. As far as I was concerned, she had answered every question adequately, so I assumed that my mother was as enthusiastic about this opportunity as I was.

Not so.

"Our family doesn't make decisions on the spot," my mother informed the woman. "We discuss things and then decide. We'll let you know after we talk about it as a family."

"But M—," I started.

"You know the rule," my mother interrupted. "And I see no reason to make an exception."

Of course I knew the rule, but this was the first time it had affected something as important as my entire future. Rules were okay for minor things, but this opportunity was too important to miss because of some arbitrary rule.

But mother had spoken, and I watched silently as the woman

stuffed my future back into her briefcase. She thanked us for our time, said she hoped to hear from us and made her way quietly down our driveway, her spike heels sinking into the dust with every step.

I left too, but not quietly. I stomped off to my room and pouted for the rest of the evening. We never did get around to discussing "as a family" my once-in-a-lifetime opportunity, but I don't think my mother was surprised. She knew me better than I thought she did—even better, of course, than I knew myself. She knew that within twenty-four hours I would lose interest in what, at that moment, I considered the opportunity of a lifetime.

I suspect that the other woman knew this about me also, but not because of any extraordinary insight on her part. She knew it because I was no different from every other starry-eyed, sixteen-year-old girl. I believed in fantasies. I believed that happiness was something you had to catch—like the bride's bouquet at a wedding—not something you had to work hard to achieve.

The difference between my mother and the other woman that day was this: although they both knew the same information about me, they used it in drastically different ways. The woman who tried to add me to her roster of recruits wanted to use my fickleness for her own advantage; her goal was to exploit my weakness. The goal of the woman who loved me was to protect me from my weakness. The woman who wanted to sell me an opportunity was thinking about her own future; the woman who loved me was thinking about my future. The woman who tried to use me for her own well-being wanted to do so by keeping my fantasies alive; the woman who loved me wanted to see my fantasies turn into reality.

The lesson my mother taught that day was this: impulsive decisions are inevitably stupid because what I want at any given moment seldom bears any resemblance to what I will want in ten years, in ten months—and sometimes even in ten minutes.

I wish I could say that I was wise beyond my years and that I learned the lesson that day and have never since sacrificed future happiness on the altar of immediate desire. But I can't. I have ignored the lesson on many occasions. I can say, however, that my goal these days is to follow it as well as I can because it has proven to be universally true. Whenever I have taken the quick and easy way and have given in to the temptation to gratify immediate desire, my only reward has been regret. On the other hand, whenever I have imagined what the future would look like if I made a particular choice, and have chosen to delay gratification, I have been rewarded with happiness.

My mother's wisdom has kept me from making serious mistakes in the major areas of life, and it continues to guide me today.

The temptation to take shortcuts to happiness (or to encourage others to do so) does not diminish with age. Every day I am tempted to settle for pleasure now at the expense of joy later.

I am tempted to buy clothes and jewelry to make myself look good rather than exercise the self-control that will make me become good. I am tempted to eat junk food to make myself feel good for a moment rather than fruits and vegetables that will make me feel good in the future. I am tempted to waste time sleeping in, watching late-night television, or surfing the internet to get momentary relief from life's pressures rather than gain lasting relief by finishing the work that is causing the pressure. I am tempted to make myself feel important by getting people to listen to my opinions rather than become important by getting involved in their lives and making my life a good example. I am tempted to go through the motions of Christianity for the satisfaction of having people think I am spiritual rather than do the hard work of prayer and meditation that will actually increase my spiritual intimacy with God.

Although I do not always win over these temptations, I am always aware of the loss I suffer when I give in to them. Thanks to my mother's early influence and training, and to several bad experiences that have reinforced her training, I am always on guard against giving in to impulsive desires.

Julie Ackerman Link is an editor for Blue Water Inc., as well as an author. Her most recent book, *The Someone Cares Encyclopedia of Letter Writing*, is published by *Guideposts Magazine*. Julie and her husband Jay live in Grand Rapids, Michigan. Julie's mother, Arlene Ackerman, worked throughout her children's teenage years as the administrative assistant to the principal at the public high school in Fruitport, Michigan. She is currently active in her church and Sunday school.

Chapter Thirty-Seven

SO MANY PEOPLE TO PRAY FOR
by Mary White

For the last ten years of her life, my mother's health declined steadily because of a rare illness. Finally, she was unable to leave her bed. She spent long hours alone as my father worked during the day and pastored a small church in the evenings and on the weekends.

By this time I was a young wife, mother of two and living across the country from my parents. I often thought of my mother, alone much of the time. I longed to be with her, to talk with her, to feed her, to read to her, to help in any way I could to fill her long quiet days.

Then one day my father wrote saying, "I thought you would like to know what your mother said to me today as I returned from work: 'Carl, are you home already? The days pass so quickly. There are so many people to pray for.'"

That attitude summarizes my mother's outlook on life. I had always admired my mother, but that comment made my admiration soar even higher. My worried heart eased as I thought of my mother spending the swiftly passing hours in prayer. I knew that my husband and I and our children were always included in those prayers.

My mother, Amy Knutson, descended from strong spiritual roots. Notes and diaries from her teen years reveal a keen interest in Bible study and sharing her faith. She actively participated in many church youth activities. She used her instrumental and vocal musical gifting in church settings. Even at that young age she loved to pray. *There are so many people to pray for....*

My mother chose the teaching profession after her high school graduation and attended "normal school," a teaching preparatory college, before going on to Northwestern Bible College in Minneapolis, where she met my father. Many of the graduates of Northwestern entered the pastorate (like my father did) or devoted their lives to missions. I met many of those pastors and missionaries in our home over the years and heard my parents pray for them frequently in our daily family devotional time. *There are so many people to pray for....*

Following graduation from Northwestern, Mother spent a year in the Ozarks conducting Bible classes in small country schools, teaching Bible studies in homes, and organizing small Sunday schools in the remote rural communities. Before she left the Ozarks to return to Minnesota to marry my dad, the women of the community made her a patchwork quilt embroidered with their names. Mother talked of these women for the rest of her life. *There are so many people to pray for....*

My older brother and I joined the family during the years of Dad's first pastorate. Some of the strongest memories I have of my mom during those days are of her natural and deep love for Jesus. Mother loved to read the Bible. On Sunday afternoons she would occasionally lie down for a rest. If I peeked in to see her, she would either be reading her Bible or sleeping with her open Bible in hand. She prayed often and with complete faith that God was listening and would answer. *There are so many people to pray for....*

Parenting is mostly demonstration with bits and pieces of specific teaching and instruction tossed in. Children observe and imitate. When I analyze my present life of prayer, I find that my mother's example still guides my life today.

My mother epitomized the truth of Philippians 2:3—"Each of you should look not only to your own interests, but also to the interests of others." Although she was busy rearing five children, she found time to serve her neighbors.

I would often accompany my mother when she visited ill neighbors. I remember one day helping her wash the hair of a woman unable to leave her bed. We visited the elderly, the sick, the blind. Mother would often play the piano and sing. She would read the Bible and pray with them. We would take the food we prepared for them.

Mother and Dad often shared hospitality with the lonely, the poor, furloughing missionaries, friends, family. Years after the fact, I found that Mother had helped a young woman attend Bible college. No fanfare, no accolades, simply a desire to help other people. And she prayed for every person she helped. *There are so many people to pray for....*

I realize it is easy to eulogize someone who is no longer living, but as I recall my mother, I remember the way she lived—her prayers, gentleness, laughter, goodness, generosity, and sympathy. But she made her strongest impact on my life as her own life ebbed away. I watched the courage and grace she displayed as she faced adversity and an uncertain future. I saw her take joy in small things, and encourage others even as she herself faced great discouragements.

I *never* heard a word of complaint from my mother about the limitations her illness imposed on her. She never mentioned the indignity of her illness or her growing dependency on others. Instead, she seemed to have a growing capacity to enjoy the simple things of life—the smile of a tiny grandchild, hearing Scripture read, quiet talks with her husband, Christian radio programs. Her advancing illness gradually robbed her of the ability to speak clearly, but her mind remained alert and keen. *There are so many people to pray for....*

As I watched her increasing physical helplessness, the narrowing of her once active life, and the growing dependency on others to care for her where she had once cared so graciously for others, I was humbled by her concern for family and friends. She could have railed and complained about her fate, made everyone around her feel guilty and miserable, and demanded constant attention, but she followed the pattern she had set years earlier and considered others more than herself.

Was she a saint? No, but close. As her life shrank to one room, her outlook seemed to broaden and sweeten. *There are so many people to pray for....*

She left a legacy of love—for people and for the Lord. She connected with people and she connected with God. And she brought them together in prayer. *There are so many people to pray for....*

Mary White is a writer and a staff member with the Navigators, of which her husband Jerry is president. Mary's latest book, *Harsh Grief, Gentle Hope*, is published by NavPress. Her mother, Amy Ethel Knutson was a teacher and a music leader in the church where her husband pastored.

CHAPTER THIRTY-EIGHT

BEAUTIFUL HANDS
by Lisa Tawn Bergren

*M*y mother doesn't have model hands. But to me, they're beautiful, even though they are freckled and beginning to show the ravages of arthritis. On her ring finger, she wears her original wedding band with a modest diamond, even though many of her friends have gone on to bigger stones. It seems she and Dad always had something better to spend their money on—usually something for us kids—college educations, cars, weddings....

Over the years, Mother's hands have done a thousand things for me. Everything from sewing Girl Scout patches on my uniforms, to braiding my hair, to writing special notes on napkins and sticking them into my lunch.

Mom's hands kneaded bread and baked countless batches of cookies and made creative cakes for birthday parties. Her hands cooled my forehead when I was burning up with fever. When the sermons in church got long, her fingers would scratch my back, sending delightful chills up my neck, calming me and keeping me from fidgeting. She'd fold her hands with mine and say prayers with me at night. It was Mom and Dad who laid their hands upon my head in prayer when I confirmed my faith in Jesus. At times, those same hands would be clasped in prayer as she beseeched the Father to show me his ways.

Mother used those beautiful hands to drive me to countless practices, and her hands clapped, cheered me on at all my games, graduations, recitals, and plays. Sometimes her hands were scorekeeper hands while I played softball, tennis, and soccer.

Mom's hands held me close when my heart was broken over some disappointing love. And when Tim, the man who would later be my husband, came along, she held out her hand in friendly greeting, welcoming him into our family like there was nothing to fear—although I'm sure she worried about me being hurt again.

With capable hands, Mom stretched out my dream wedding gown, checking to make sure everything was just right. With nimble fingers, she drew the veil over my face on our wedding day as she smiled into my eyes. Even though I'm sure it was tough, she waved good-bye, letting me go to find my own way. Later, her hands cradled our new daughter, loving her as only a doting grandmother can.

Mother's hands spent a lifetime shaping me. Her sculpting through careful attention, consistent love, and steady interest in my growth prepared me for life—and for celebrating life's best. With her hands, she showed me how to be a good mother and now I have the chance to emulate her work with my own daughter.

I know many other mothers have used their hands in such beautiful ways for their daughters. But to me, my mother's hands are extraordinary. When I was a kid and she'd dress up to go out, I'd sit on her bed, watching cross-legged as she got ready. I thought she looked like a movie star.

But I see her beauty differently now. It is a quiet, dignified glow—the kind of beauty that comes from a lifetime of learning, laughing, and loving. It is my hope that with time, when my daughter sees my rough hands with unmanicured nails, she'll see past the imperfections to the strength, love, and constancy that are in them, too.

Lisa Tawn Bergen is Executive Editor of Fiction for WaterBrook Press, as well as a successful fiction writer. She makes her home in Colorado Springs with her husband Tim, a liturgical sculptor, and daughter Olivia. Lisa's mother, Karen Grosswiler was an R.N. and now spends much of her retirement time in Bible study and as a caregiver through her church's Stephen's Ministry program.

CHAPTER THIRTY-NINE

LOVE IS SLOW

by Mary Jenson

Underneath Mom's new Nancy Reagan wig was a bald head I hadn't yet seen. Her smart clothes had been left behind. Shuffling down the airport corridor with my sister, she looked like someone else's elderly mother—T-shirt and sweater, sweat pants, sneakers and sport socks—slower in step and with a dimness that belied her natural enthusiasm. I obviously couldn't fling my arms around her neck and start my customary nonstop chatter; nor could I sneak up behind her and surprise her as I might have in the past. For the first time in my life she was fragile, porcelain, opalescent.

Waving to give plenty of warning, I walked toward them, willing the moistness out of my eyes. "Hi, you sweet thing," I nuzzled in her neck. My sister and I exchanged knowing looks, the kind mothers share over their children's heads.

And so began our last four months together.

Mom came to my home in California for seven weeks that summer to give my sisters a respite from her care, and to help me understand what they and she were going through. It was an eye-opener.

Her non-Hodgkins lymphoma had recently spread undetected to her brain. There it pushed aside short-term memory and the ability to perform certain habitual tasks we take for granted.

Numerous little oddities defined each day. Mom set the table with three forks at this place, two knives and a spoon at that one. She poured orange juice into the coffee thermos and wrapped drippy watermelon in paper towels to store in the refrigerator.

Putting on her bra became a group activity.

Despite her advancing cancer, she was in good health that summer—except for one little virus, which required daily doses of ear drops. Each time, she had to relearn how to hold that bottle and get the drops in her ear. Those were very frustrating moments—moments when her neurologist's reprimand came painfully to mind: "Remember, she's doing the best she can."

Everything we did that summer took longer than I thought it would. Mom gave simple tasks the same weight as weekend forays to the mountains. I wrestled with my impatience, astonished and embarrassed that this woman, this mother, could elicit any emotion from me other than affection. I tapped my foot inside my head, all the while reminding myself that love is slow.

She went back to Denver in September. I think I knew she would die soon. I wish, I wish, we could have talked about death. For years we had talked about everything else. We had shared laughter so unrelenting I would have to leave the room to breathe. We shared confidences, prayers, hopes, jokes, books, recipes, and politics. We could have talked about death as well, but now, watching her puzzled look about everyday trivia, I knew it would be too much for her. I wanted to tell her that everything would be okay. That my two sisters and I would be able to handle this transition in all our lives. That dying is part of everything we are. That the God we both had confessed is no dream but a real Being who was orchestrating her last months and waiting eagerly for her arrival.

Mom spent her last two weeks in the home of one of my sisters with almost constant attendance from one of us or our aunt, who helped us with the decisions, daily struggles, and administration that are a part of dying. The last few nights we bunked in her room, curled in chairs or on sleeping bags.

Mother died in our sleep.

At seven o'clock that morning we three sisters and our aunt took what we later called "The Walk." Marching like Rockettes down the middle of the street, we dared any motorist to break us up, exulting in the early morning crispness, relieved for ourselves and Mom that the ordeal was over. We sang, we laughed, we cried, we walked in silence, breathing deeply, arms locked all the way.

The day of her funeral was beautiful. Colorado in November—and, strangely enough, the air still warm, the grass still green, and many fall leaves still bright on the trees. Clouds like beaten egg whites scudded across the sky; geese wandered among the gravestones at the cemetery. The memorial service was a joyful one. The sanctuary filled with friends who loved her, who laughed along with us at remembrances of funny things that had happened to her or witticisms she had offered. It was a grand send-off, the embodiment of Psalm 30:11—"You turned my wailing into dancing; You removed my sackcloth and clothed me in joy."

I was forty-one years old when Mom died—too young to lose a mother. Now, six years later, I can't hear her voice in my mind anymore. That disturbs me. My memory of her face, sustained by photographs, is still clouded by the last weeks of her life, when her eyes were blank and her skin lifeless, like a peach past its freshness.

I miss the banter, the laughter, the friendship, the way she routinely ended our phone calls with, "Bye honey. I love you." I miss shopping with her, sitting together and talking with our feet stretched out in front of us, and the way she scratched my back when I was little—and not so little. I miss having someone interested in anything and everything I have to say. I ache to ask her how she handled her empty nest now that mine's so imminent.

But I feel her presence when I wrap my arms around my children like she did around me. I catch a glimpse of her face when I walk quickly past a store window and see her in my thin straight hair and slightly bowed legs. I recognize her words in my own and revel in the memory of our rich communication. Some women say with regret, "I'm becoming my mother." I'll never be her, but I'm working hard at being as like her as I can.

Mary Jenson is Ron's wife and mother to Matt and Molly. Her first book, *Partners in Promise*, was published in 1996, and she's hard at work on more. She credits her mother, Missy Kunz, with showing her an uncompromising, unequaled, unconditional, unflappable, undying love.

CHAPTER FORTY

A MOTHER'S DAY THANKS
by Mayo Mathers

*M*rs. Mathers? I'm calling to let you know we've accepted your son's rental application. He can move in anytime."

The words set my emotions at war: excitement for Tyler, sadness for me.

My nineteen-year-old son began packing immediately, anticipation in every movement. As I helped, my mind whirled: *He doesn't have enough money...his car doesn't run very well...he doesn't have furniture....*

A gigantic list formed in my mind. *Tyler's going to need groceries, towels, blankets, pans, dishes, money....* Weren't these necessities? I had to provide them.

Suddenly, in the middle of my thoughts careened the word *STOP*. I jerked around, startled, then stopped and went to my bedroom. *Lord, what are you telling me?*

As I pondered the strange command, I thought back to when I'd been nineteen. I'd packed my suitcase and boarded a train for Portland, Oregon. I didn't have a job, a place to live, or anyone to contact when I arrived. I spent my first night at the YMCA, then walked around downtown Portland looking for a job and an apartment. I found both within a few days.

Those first weeks on my own, I used my coat for a blanket, a T-shirt for a towel, and ate food that didn't require cooking. For me, it was high adventure. The independence was exhilarating. The voice in my head now said, *The greatest gift your mother gave you was that independence.*

Not long ago, my mother told me how upset she'd been by my move. "There was no one in Portland who could watch out for you. No way I could even make sure you were safe!" I had laughed when she told me that. Now I wasn't laughing.

My mother had resisted protecting me and instead allowed me to find my own way in the world. She hadn't insisted on going with me to find a "suitable" apartment, nor had she loaded me down with "necessities." She waved good-bye with no strings attached. Now it was my turn.

Walking back into Tyler's room, I mentally tore up my list of "musts."

However, recognizing the value of Mom's gift—and being able to pass it on to Tyler—was easier said than done. As we packed up the last of his things on the day he moved out, I saw him silently looking around his room. I smiled, "Is it strange to leave the only home you've ever known?"

"Yeah, it's weird to see my room empty."

I wanted to smother him with a hug and say, "Oh, Tyler! You don't have to move out!" The words were on the tip of my tongue, but I held them back. Instead I touched his arm. "Tyler, the whole world's waiting. God's plan is already unfolding, and you have so much to look forward to."

A few minutes later, as I watched his car disappear down the road, I realized a door had shut that would never again open. Grief filled my heart, but I thought again of my mother's strength and wisdom. Her gift of independence gave me the strength I now needed to let go. I smiled through my tears. *Thanks, Mom.*

Mayo Mathers is a contributing editor for *Today's Christian Woman* magazine, a freelance writer, and a speaker with Stonecroft Ministries of Kansas City. She is the mother of two grown sons. Her mother, Zell Randall, is a recently retired teacher and farmer's wife. These days she can be found traveling through the United States with her husband, who is also recently retired.

(Reprinted from an article appearing in *Today's Christian Woman*, May/June 1996. Used with permission.)

CHAPTER FORTY-ONE

AS MOTHERLY AS APPLE PIE
by Melissa Morris McBurney

*H*anging in one of the bedrooms at the Marble Retreat, which my husband and I run, is an antique photograph of a beautiful young girl. She was sweet sixteen and the "sponsor" of the Longview Lobos football team. She was a knockout—dark hair and beautiful dark eyes. I have always thought, although I don't know for sure, that the "sponsor" was the same as football queen or sweetheart. I don't think they even have such things nowadays. That picture is of Minnie Frances Williams, my mother. She is still very attractive at ninety years of age, and if North 15th Street had a football team, she would still be chosen "sponsor."

Mother has always been a favorite. People want to be around her, she is so much fun. When we talk on the phone, my husband, Louis, is always curious because he hears lots of laughter. Even experiences that most people would see as negative—being forgetful, or taking a wrong turn and getting lost, or having a skunk under her house—she sees with humor.

Louis and I live in the Rocky Mountains and in our valley we have no TV reception. That's sometimes hard for our visitors who want to know what is going on in the world. But the last time Mother visited us in Colorado, she learned to use my computer so she could play solitaire and find out the latest on her TV programs. She was so proud to go home and tell her friends that she was now computer literate.

I have always admired Mother's willingness to try something new. During her first winter visit to Marble she tried on a pair of skis. She didn't go further than the driveway but at least she got the feel. A few years later when she was seventy-two years old, she went river rafting on the Colorado River with us.

Mother's adventurousness and fun-loving personality are precious to me, but they are not the main reason I feel so blessed to have her as my mother. The best part of being Minnie's daughter is that she taught me common sense, values that have made my life rich and full, wisdom about people and their feelings, how important family is, what loyalty is all about, a reasonable attitude about responsibility, and how to make a great apple pie.

It is hard to put my finger on exactly *how* she taught me those things. I know that she taught me to be unprejudiced and to respect the differences in others. She grew up in Texas during a time when prejudice was a way of life—and her family was certainly one with that culture. It is rumored that some members of the family were even in the KKK. But somehow, Mother rejected that racist viewpoint and I was taught a healthy respect for all people.

Mother is still a product of her times—times that were considerate and gracious. Her dentist said recently that she was one of the last "real ladies." Learning those ways of behaving have made my life much easier. Consideration and graciousness oil the wheels of relationships in a wonderful way.

Looking back on my relationship with Mother, I can see how God has used an earthly relationship to teach me how to relate to him. Mother used to say that when I was a child all she had to do was give me a stern look and I obeyed. I certainly knew that she meant business and that disobedience was not a good choice for me. Of course, I didn't always obey. Once I went on an outing with friends—even though Mother had forbidden it because she knew I would get poison ivy from the place we were going. Sure enough, I got poison ivy and then tried to cover my sin. I went to a different doctor to get the medicine thinking Mother would never know. However, I forgot to take the medicine home and the nurse called and let the cat out of the bag.

Minnie had learned the same lesson about obedience from her

mother. When she was in college, the rules for "young ladies" were very strict. Once she wanted to go on a weekend trip with a group of friends but had used all her passes. She sent a telegram to her mother suggesting that if her mother were "sick" she would be allowed to go. "Please send a telegram to the Dean asking for me to come home." Mother packed and waited outside the Dean's office for the telegram to arrive. It did. It said, "Am feeling much better—no need to come."

I see now that my mother's own training made it much easier for me, as I watched her, to learn how to obey the Lord. I have seen many people who never learn obedience as children, and as adults, they find it difficult to obey God.

Knowing Mother's love was always there for me also helped me to recognize that God's love would always be there for me. I learned that sometimes love is tough and not all warm and fuzzy. It doesn't always look like we want it to. Knowing this, I understood why God's love is sometimes difficult to receive.

When I was in college and engaged to a young seminary student, just a month before our wedding, he and I were in a car wreck. Mother, who had a history of fainting at the sight of blood, was right there for me in the ambulance ride to the hospital, even though I was a bloody mess. Ernie died that night from his injuries, and again Mother was there to help me reconcile this tragedy with God's love for me. Just as she was there for me, so was God. It was one of the most real experiences I have had with God. The pain was overwhelmed by the power of His presence and love. I could trust in my mother's love *and* God's love.

Not only did God give me a good, wise and fun mother; He gave me a mother who can make great apple pies!

Here is her favorite recipe:

> Six pie apples, peeled and grated using the largest holes on the grater
> Lots of butter in little pats
> Lots of sugar to sprinkle around
> Cinnamon
> One pie shell (uncooked)

Layer half of the grated apples in the pie shell, sprinkle with half the sugar and cinnamon. Put little pats of butter on top. Start on the next layer of apples, sugar and cinnamon with little pats of butter around the top. Make some pie dough strips and lattice them on the top. Be sure to make it pretty! Bake in a 350-degree oven until nicely brown.

Disclaimer: this recipe comes from a time before fat grams were even known and may be hazardous to your diet. But then, my mother is still living at age ninety. So what can I say about her hazardous apple pies?

Melissa Morris McBurney lives in Marble, Colorado, and is the co-therapist, bookkeeper, and secretary for Marble Retreat, a psychotherapy center for ministers and their spouses. Melissa's mother, Minnie Williams Morris, will celebrate her ninetieth birthday this year in Temple, Texas, where she lives.

CHAPTER FORTY-TWO

HARD TIME, HARD WORK, HARD PLACES
by Florence Littauer

My mother was a fragile woman. She was 5'6" tall but she weighed less than 100 pounds when she got married. It seemed my father's aim was to keep her healthy. I grew up thinking she was weak, but really, she was very strong emotionally. She had to be, considering all she had to face in life.

My mother was raised in a comfortable middle-class home where all seven children had advanced education. She studied music in Boston, and she and her sister had a studio together where they taught music— my aunt, piano; my mother, violin. At age twenty-eight, my mother married my father, who was forty-eight, and they settled into that typical little white house with the picket fence. They had all new furniture and wedding presents from all her pupils. My father had a secure job and they looked forward to retiring on a pension someday.

But then, the Depression hit. The business my father worked for collapsed. The country was in the pits economically and my father lost everything. Finding himself at age sixty with three small children and a discouraged wife, my father borrowed $2000 dollars to open a small grocery store. It was called the Riverside Variety Store. The store was open from 6:30 A.M. to 11 p.m. and my mother worked day and night in the store.

We lived in the three small rooms behind the store. My two brothers and I, my mother, and my father slept stacked on bunks in one room. The other two rooms were kitchen and sitting room. I'm sure it was hard on my mother's pride, but she went to charity centers just to see that we had clothing and food.

Most of what I remember about my mother was that she worked all the time. She never had time even to decorate the rooms we lived in. When I was fifteen and went to work selling chocolates, one of the first things I did was to buy white dish towels with strawberries on them and thumb-tack them over the windows so we would at least have curtains. We had worn out linoleum on the floor, so I bought some paint and sponge painted it yellow with blotches of red and white.

For all the drudgery in her life, my mother did see to it that we kept up with our music and that I went on with my elocution lessons. She moved her piano into the tiny sitting room, and there she taught us music. My brother Ron learned to play the trumpet, and brother Jim took singing lessons. Sunday evenings we would gather in the sitting room for hymn sings. Mother played her violin, I played the piano and Ron played the trumpet. My brother Jim led the singing. Customers would hear the hymns and often joined us in the tiny room.

I don't remember my mother being particularly joyful through all the hard times, but I do remember that she never complained. She was always lovely—always gracious and pleasant to everyone. The customers loved her. She taught us by her example how to be polite and nice to people no matter who they were. In the store, we couldn't be critical or we would lose customers. So, early on, I learned the importance of social graces and a compassionate attitude.

Since Mother was always in the store, the store became our second home. We played there, did our homework there, worked there. My father, who was born and raised in England, had a great love for the English language. He had always been above average in all his pursuits. And even now, when he had nothing materially, he and Mother were always there for us. We were never alone, never felt rejected or ignored. We never came home to an empty house.

Though my mother and I were nothing alike (I am more like my Aunt Jean), I greatly admire the fact that in adverse circumstances—which she really didn't deserve—Mother didn't complain. She accepted her lot in life and was a peaceful person. In the midst of a very negative situation, she raised us to be positive, productive, and creative people, all successful in our own concerns.

As a child growing up, I never really knew how much Mother had to tolerate. I'm sure, even now I do not appreciate it all. She lost all her financial security in her early thirties. She worked like a "drudge" in a grocery store for most of her years when she would like to have been teaching violin. She was widowed at age fifty. Despite it all, she was able to rise above and show us children that we could do something with our lives in spite of our circumstances.

Mother died at age eighty-five. Looking back, I wish I had been more in tune to her feelings in her later years. I took good care of her, but I think I could have done more for her if I'd just realized how she felt. She was so quiet, and I didn't pry below the surface.

For example, I wish I'd seen to it that she had a chance to play her violin. I wish I'd asked her if she were feeling lonely, or if she felt nobody needed her anymore. The irony is that the older I get, the more I understand how my mother must have felt.

Today, I still have the first small violin my mother played. She started playing violin when she was four years old, and later added the cello and bag pipes. Her name wasn't Katie MacDougall for nothing! My mother's violin is a reminder to me of a talented woman who, through no fault of her own, went backwards in life as far as material possessions are concerned, and yet was able to carry on important family traditions such as music and drama—traditions that enabled her children to develop their own gifts and identities.

Florence Littauer is a highly respected motivational speaker, author, and the founder and president of CLASS Speakers, Inc. She has written more than twenty books, including the bestsellers *Dare to Dream*, *Silver Boxes* and *Personality Plus*. Florence's mother was Katie Florence MacDougall, who was born in Halifax, Nova Scotia, and later moved to the United States.

CHAPTER FORTY-THREE

MOM'S GIFT OF ENCOURAGEMENT
by Marita Littauer

*A*fter teaching a recent seminar with my mother, Florence Littauer, I received a note from one of our attendees that said, "Congratulations Marita. I have seen many ministries and businesses where the parent is the leader and a child is involved. You have been able to maintain your own identity while complementing the talents of your mother. This is not easy to do and I admire you for it."

While I was pleased to receive this comment, it caused me to reflect on the history that led up to such a statement being made.

Looking back, I can see that I truly am who I am today because of the years my mother invested in me. I have two siblings, an older sister and a younger brother, but I am the one who has always had an interest in my mother's world—the world of Christian speaking and writing. We began to work together when I was only thirteen.

The invitations for my mother to speak at Christian women's clubs and smaller church women's retreats were just beginning to come in. She had basically been a "full-time mom" during our childhood, but as we grew, so did she. I began to go with her to some of her events.

When I was fifteen, Mom and Emilie Barnes teamed up to teach a woman's seminar. I remember going to those seminars. My main job was to pass out the papers they were using for each session. After teaching their seminars locally, they were invited to teach one over a weekend in northern California.

The three of us flew to Castro Valley and rented a Ford Pinto to drive to a hotel and the church where the seminar was held. Between the three of us, we only had six dollars in cash for dinner (I guess Mother and Emilie didn't have their own credit cards at that time). During one of the sessions, my mother taught on the subject of depression. She announced to the ladies that she had a Bible study on the topic in the back, and that if they were interested they should see me at the break.

These "Bible studies" were two or three typewritten pages, photocopied on pale green paper and stapled together. We usually sold them for twenty-five cents each. But since we were really low on money, I figured if the women would pay twenty-five cents, they would pay fifty. I sold them all!

When it was time for dinner that night, my mother and Emilie were lamenting our plight and trying to figure out where we could go for six dollars. I held up the Bible study money and said, "We have depression money. We can go anywhere!" While we couldn't truly go anywhere, we did have more options! From that time on, my role was cast. I began to participate more often in my mother's ministry.

When I was nineteen and in college, like most nineteen-year-olds, I did not know what I wanted to do with my life. Though I was majoring in interior design, I wasn't sure it was the field for me. I discussed the situation with my mother. My search for what to do with my life coincided with my mother's and Emilie's search for someone to fill a need in their program—the idea of "having your colors done" as a means for organizing a wardrobe.

My mother said to me one day, "Marita, you have a good eye for color, you like working with people, and you enjoy traveling with Emilie and me. Why don't you learn to do this color analysis and come work with us?"

My mother had seen some gifts and abilities in me, and she gave me opportunity to use them. Before long, I was working with my mother and talking to women about the topics of color, wardrobe, and make-up.

Before long, a book company asked me to put together a book on the topic. I didn't know if I could write, but again my mother came to my side and encouraged that gift in me. Just like she'd done when I was a kid writing school reports, she helped me re-write and edit as I wrote the book.

Today, at age thirty-eight, my color analysis business is a thing of the past. But those early years of traveling and working with my mother, of having her encourage different gifts in me, have had a deep and lasting impact on my present. Over the past ten years, I've continued to work side by side with my mother. She has shaped me and trained me in many areas. She has given me the tools I needed to become the person God intended for me to be. And she has done it all without pushing me to be who she may have wanted me to be. For that I am very thankful.

Marita Littauer is a speaker, author and organizer, and a contributing editor to the *Christian Communicator Magazine*, which is the trade publication for Christian speakers and writers. Marita is also co-founder of the CLASSeminar, and the chairman and founder of the Southern California Women's Retreat. Marita is the daughter of popular speaker and author Florence Littauer.

CHAPTER FORTY-FOUR

MY MOTHER THE SPY
by Jane Johnson Struck

Outwardly, I appear to be a mild-mannered suburban housewife who car pools, irons, parks myself in front of a computer monitor for my part-time job, and attends church faithfully. But there's a hidden side to me that's always secretly desired to be a dashing private investigator or police detective. I'd always chalked this interest up to a steady childhood diet of Nancy Drew mysteries or the hours I spent in the '60s watching popular television series such as the *Man from U.N.C.L.E.* or *The Avengers.* I imagined myself becoming a glamorous Cold War spy or a crack sleuth who solved cases with her stunning intuitive abilities. Reality, however, turned out nothing like my childhood fantasies!

But then, a few months ago, I received startling insight into my fascination with the world of intrigue. My mom and dad made the six-hour drive out from Michigan to visit our family for a few days. As we sat on the couch, chatting comfortably over diet colas to catch up on life, our conversation, not surprisingly, turned to the latest political controversy over the apparent mishandling of FBI files.

"You know," Mom said suddenly, "I always wanted to be a spy when I was growing up."

Say *what?*

"I even took a bus to the FBI headquarters in Chicago and filled out an application, but they never called me for an interview," she continued. "I think they thought I was too young. So there's probably an FBI file on me somewhere."

My mom—a secret agent wanna-be? Never before had I heard this tantalizing tidbit of information about my mother's adolescence. While our chitchat turned to other things, inwardly I was jolted with the realization that I wasn't as unique as I had fancied! It dawned on me: *if such a thing as a detective gene exists, I've surely inherited them from my mother.*

Sleuthing aside, I've always known I inherited many of my mom's emotional traits. We're both melodramatic at times, highly verbal, creative, sensitive. I've inherited many of Mom's physical traits as well—too-youthful skin, generous hips, and a zesty appetite (especially for sweets). In fact, when I was a teen and my mom and I were together—at church, the grocery store, the mall—people often remarked on how we looked like sisters. At the time, I wasn't sure how I felt about those comments; they often irked me. But now, from my vantage point as a forty-something mother with two teenage daughters, I completely understand how those compliments must have made my mother's day!

But it's Mom's passion for family—caring about what each one's going through, taking the time to pen handwritten letters in this discourteous, letterless age—that's shaped me the most. Whatever knack I may have for encouraging others through short notes, whatever common courtesy and thoughtfulness I try to express, I owe to my mom's caring example.

A poignant reminder of the significance of my mom's ability to care and encourage occurred just days ago when I cried on the phone long-distance to her, frightened about a medical test I would undergo the next day while my husband was out of town. I was very anxious about the outcome: "I'm scared the results will be bad and I'll be all alone," I sobbed into the telephone.

"You're never alone, Jane," my mother told me calmly, lovingly. "Remember, God is always with you." How I needed to be reminded of exactly that at exactly that moment! And how wonderful that my mom could be the one to remind me.

In addition, Mom's pursuit of our family roots has enriched my life by providing me with a sense of belonging to family in a larger, grander sense. Mom's genealogical detective work (maybe "the spy" coming out in her) has unearthed a wealth of information on family members long gone. She's taken the time and made the effort to make sense of what otherwise would remain a puzzling jumble of names and dates. The end result? I've been given a strong sense of identity, of continuity, of connection to a community of ancestors long gone. Mom's gift to me is this wonderful sense of heritage, of belonging, which I hope to pass on to my children.

As I grow older, and *wiser*—I'd like to think—I continually recognize and appreciate more aspects of my mother's influence. Many of these insights become clear only as I falteringly and prayerfully mother my own two daughters through adolescence. When I was in my teens, there were many times I told myself that when I was married and had kids, I would be different from my mom—less protective, more relaxed about the house, less mercurial. Yet somehow, with the births of my daughters, my relationship with Mom has evolved from one of stubborn desire for independence to one of respect and growing admiration. Now, when someone tells me I'm just like my mom, I take it as the highest compliment.

Jane Johnson Struck is an associate editor for *Today's Christian Woman Magazine*, and the mother of two teenage daughters. She resides in Wheaton, Illinois. Her mother, Janet Johnson, is the church clerk at Farmington Hills Baptist Church in Farmington Hills, Michigan. She also leads the seniors' group at the church. When mother and daughter get together they enjoy playing miniature golf, shopping, and going to Dairy Queen.

CHAPTER FORTY-FIVE

MONEY DOESN'T GROW ON TREES...
AND OTHER WISE SAYINGS FROM MY MOTHER
by Kathy Troccoli

My mother died of cancer. I've often thought about how courageous she was during the time of her illness. She handled the dying process with such dignity and humility. During all the prodding, poking, and surgery she never once complained. Toward the end, all I heard was an occasional, "I'm getting tired."

In her healthier days, Mom was known for her funny phrases. She often used classics like "Money doesn't grow on trees" and "Well it's all fun and games until someone gets hurt!" But beyond all the humorous phrases Mom would say, she gave me some serious gems I still cherish.

Right before my eyes she lived out another of her famous phrases: "God will give you strength when you need it." When I went through the hardest, darkest times of my life—days of struggling and tears—she gave me those tender words. And as the ravages of cancer took over her body, I saw my mother cling to that very promise.

Out of everything my mother ever said to me, I think that statement has meant the most. "God will give you strength when you need it." It's true. I've seen the Lord meet me time and time again when I desperately needed it. Somehow He gave me the grace to endure and walk through situations that seemed unbearable. Now I realize as I look back on those tough times, how present Jesus really was.

There are many phrases my mother used to say when I was growing up. Some of them I still laugh about with friends. My sister and I often remind each other of those bold "words of wisdom" she would often quote to us. But in the last years since Mother's death, I have come to be comforted by those very phrases. For the truth of the matter is that my mother wasn't only speaking her heart...she was also speaking the heart of God.

Kathy Troccoli is a well-known Christian musician, with seven albums and ten number one songs to her name. Her most recent album is *Sounds of Heaven*. Kathy is also an author. Her first book will be released from Zondervan Publishing House this spring. Her mother, Josephine Troccoli, was a secretary to the superintendent of the Public School District in Long Island, New York. Kathy's mom always believed Kathy was born to sing. While she was alive, she was Kathy's biggest fan. Even now, Kathy sometimes pictures her mother watching her as she performs.

CHAPTER FORTY-SIX

THE LEGACY OF AN OPPOSITE
by Mary Whelchel

My mother and I are opposites in most ways. In fact, I don't doubt that there have been many days in my life she has seriously wondered if she brought the wrong baby home from the hospital. And though she would never admit it, I'm equally sure there have been days she wished she could swap me for some other daughter. She has frequently admitted that I was more difficult to raise than both of my older brothers put together!

Our personalities are quite opposite: she is reserved, quiet, almost shy—a behind-the-scenes person who would never knowingly draw attention to herself. I am the up-front, take-charge person who sometimes draws far too much attention to herself. She is loved and admired by everyone and almost never gets herself into trouble. I've cleaned so much shoe polish off my face from foot-in-mouth disease that it's a wonder my face isn't permanently stained.

Our lifestyles are also at the opposite ends of the spectrum. She has lived out a traditional female role, and loved every minute of it. She married in her early twenties, raised three children, never worked outside her home, was always home for me and my brothers, took care of her husband and her house, and never thought about her need to express herself or find herself or do her own thing. She could not tell you what "self-actualization" means.

She washes on Mondays, irons on Tuesdays and cleans the house on Saturdays—as regular as clock work. She irons her sheets and Daddy's underwear and pajamas. She wouldn't know the first thing about computers or fax machines, balance sheets or strategic plans, and she would find airports and taxis and fancy restaurants intimidating and a bit frightening.

I've been a career woman since I became a single mom when my daughter was eight. I've helped break new ground for women—in the corporate world, in my church, in the world of Christian radio. I've sold computer equipment, been a director of marketing and sales and had to learn something about budgets and financial planning. I've traveled from one end of the world to the other, and I am totally comfortable in almost any environment, from corporate boardrooms to live radio call-in programs, to audiences of thousands. Non-traditional is definitely a description of my life.

And yet, though my mother cannot relate to my world in many ways, she is the godliest woman I know and my ultimate role model. There are two qualities about her which will always be her greatest legacy to me.

First is her passionate love for God's Word and the consistency of her commitment to study it, memorize it, and teach it. I've never known anyone who loved God's Word like she does. I have memories of walking into the kitchen in our simple home and finding Mom studying her Bible. Or waking and finding that Mother has gotten up before the rest of us to have her quiet time. Mother didn't have to be told to do this; she never seemed to think of it as a duty. This was the most treasured time of her day and her only regret was that she couldn't put more hours each day into Bible study. For a one-hour Sunday school class, she would spend thirty to forty hours studying.

Now that she is older and caring for my father after his stroke, she has had to give up her Sunday class—one of the most painful sacrifices she's ever made, I'm sure. But she still finds time alone with the word of God. She often shares with me what she's learning from her study, and when she does the tone of her voice changes—the weariness goes away and an invigorating passion comes through the telephone. She has memorized long passages and even whole books from the Bible, and I'm convinced that it has kept her mind alert through the years.

Many people study and acquire knowledge about the Bible, but few people love it like my mother does. As a result she has passed on to me a firm commitment to the truth of God's word and to basing every aspect of my life and my ministry on the Bible. I'll never be the student she is; I'm an exhorter, she's a teacher. But I'll always remember her passionate love of the Bible and her life-long commitment to knowing it better and better.

Secondly, my mother has taught me through example what it means to be teachable. At eighty-four, after sixty-five years of marriage, she is still trying to be a better wife. She reads anything helpful, listens to tapes and radio programs with interest, and then applies it to her life with obedience and joy.

One of her grandsons is a minister, and I remember once when she went to hear him preach. In telling me about the sermon—and of course, Grandma thought it was wonderful—she told me how his words had convicted her and how she was going to change some aspect of her attitude because of her grandson's sermon.

She listens to her daughter on the radio and God speaks to her through me—that still amazes me! I remember when she asked me to send her a copy of my prayer journal, which I publish often to help others learn how to pray and structure their prayer time more effectively. I said "Mom, you don't need my prayer journal—not you, of all people. You know how to pray better than I ever will!"

"No," she insisted, "I think it will help me."

After using it for a few weeks, she told me how God was using my ideas to help her pray better!

Teachable—that's the greatest legacy my mom has left me. And it's the greatest challenge as well. When we stay teachable, we are truly humble. We don't get mentally old. I've noticed how as Mother ages she becomes softer, more loving, and more lovable. There are so many people who love her dearly, beyond her loving family. And I'm convinced that she has grown more lovable instead of cranky and cantankerous (as we say down South) because she has always been teachable, willing to learn, willing to change, and willing to obey.

I've got a long way to go to live up to her role model, but only eternity will tell how great her influence has been on me. She is proud of my accomplishments for the Lord and amazed, as I am, at what God has allowed me to do. But of this I'm sure: whatever good I've done for the kingdom of God, it's my mother who will get a great portion of the reward.

Mary Whelchel is the founder of *The Christian Working Woman*, a radio program begun in 1984 and now broadcast through more than 500 stations across the United States and abroad. Her most recent books include *If You Only Knew*, published by Victor Books, and *How to Thrive from 9 to 5*, published by Word Publishing. Mary's mother, Irene Stiles, is a mother of three, grandmother of eight and great-grandmother of seventeen. She lives in the Chattanooga, Tennessee, area.

Chapter Forty-seven

HEAVEN'S GARDENS
by Ruth A. Tucker

In the Garden" was my mother's favorite hymn, the hymn we sang at her funeral. I often reflect on that hymn as I'm sitting under the awning on my back deck, looking out into the garden. I'm most often alone in my garden and it's a good place to reflect—on God and on memories gone by.

It's been more than a quarter of a century since my mother died, and most of the time my life goes on as if that terrible day in 1969 never happened. It was 6:30 on the evening of September 23rd, just as I turned on the NBC evening news—a moment etched forever in my memory with shock, horror, and indescribable grief. The phone rang in our tiny New Jersey apartment, and the message from my brother Jonnie conveyed the news that my mother had been killed in a car accident late that afternoon. As I hung up the phone, my words of anguish summed up the finality of that broken bond: "I can never talk to her again—never again."

As I've reflected back on that first expression of despair, I now understand why talking to Mom was so very important to me then, and why I continue to miss it so much even today. My mother was a teacher turned farmer's wife and—whether for evil or for good—she lived for us five kids. Her dream was to see us all graduate from college; we all did, but she did not live to see it. She was always proud of our accomplishments, and it was impossible to "brag" too much to her. Indeed, she would literally interrogate us about our achievements and successes. She adored her two grandchildren, and my son, Carlton, would have been the apple of her eye as well if she had lived to know him. I think of Mother on special occasions, and wish she could have known Carlton through his growing up years.

I no longer cry—except when caught by a moment that I'm not prepared for.

I thought of her tonight as I watched Sally Field starring in *A Woman of Independent Means*. Sally portrayed a woman who had lost her husband some years earlier, and her oldest son had died during the previous year. But here she was at the cemetery all day in grief over her mother who had died even longer ago. "It's strange," she lamented, "how grief doubles back on you, ambushes you."

Yes, it is strange after all these years. The wound has still not completely healed, and the grief does double back on me and ambush me when I'm least expecting it. But I will always have a garden of memories with all its color and fragrances. And when I think of heaven, I think not so much of streets of gold but of beautiful gardens—gardens far more glorious than my mother's ever were or mine ever will be.

Ruth A. Tucker is the author of twelve books, visiting professor at Trinity Evangelical Divinity School, and a widely traveled retreat and conference speaker. She makes her home in Grand Rapids, Michigan. Her mother, Jennie Carlton Stellrecht, was a farmer's wife and mother of five.

(Reprinted from the book, *Season of Motherhood, A Garden of Memories* by Victor/Chariot Books, Colorado Springs, Colorado. Used with permission.)

CHAPTER FORTY-EIGHT

A LOVE AFFAIR TO LAST A LIFETIME
by Angela Elwell Hunt

I am ten years old. It is a sultry Florida summer afternoon. School is scheduled to start next week, and I have run out of ideas to entertain myself.

"Mom, I'm bored," I say as I sit on the front porch of our house. Mom is inside fixing dinner.

"Have you finished reading the books we got from the library?" She yells over the clang of the pots and pans.

"Yesterday. Can you take me back to the library to get more?" (Going to the library is my favorite thing to do.)

Mother steps out onto the porch and fans herself with her tea towel. The heat is stifling. The sweat shines off Mom's brow.

"I'm sorry Angie. I just can't. I've got to get dinner started. You are going to have to find something to do on your own. What about that box of books in the closet? Have you looked at those?"

I haven't.

It doesn't take me long to find the box she is talking about. We discovered it when we moved into this house. It had been left from a previous owner. Today, the dusty old carton looks like a hidden pot of gold to me. *Jane Eyre, Cyrano de Bergerac*…it is filled with the classics.

Although new to me, the books feel as though they are old friends. The smell of musty pages and worn leather combine in my nose. I dig deeper to see what other riches my treasure chest holds. At the very bottom of the box, tucked away underneath all the rest, my hands touch a cool, smooth cover. I pull it out and discover *The Nun's Story* by

Kathryn Hulme. I open the cover and immediately I am lost in a world of convents and catechism, and a woman's struggle with obedience. As the shadows creep across the floor of my bedroom, I am transported to another time and another place. It is a story that captivates me completely and reaches out to touch my soul. It is a story I will keep with me forever.

Eighteen years later, shortly after the death of Kathryn Hulme, I became acquainted, through correspondence, with the woman who inspired *The Nun's Story*. I sent her a message of condolence, to which she responded, "Kathryn would have loved you."

One of the greatest gifts my mother ever gave me was a love for reading. From my earliest days, I recall books always being around the house. The *Child's Bible Reader* was my first book. It was filled with stories from the Old and New Testaments, with beautiful pictures depicting Moses, Noah, and Baby Jesus. Mom started growing her reader by sitting with me and reading the stories out loud. It didn't take long until I had the stories memorized and could read them back to her. Today, the battered copy of this book remains on my bookcase as a reminder of how my love affair with reading began.

With a family of three girls to raise, and a home to run, extra time was a luxury for my mother. Even so, she made time to take me to the library and she made sure that I was exposed to all types of books. And her encouragement worked, I didn't know many other kids who were reading *Jane Eyre* in fifth grade and *Gone with the Wind* in sixth!

There is no doubt in my mind that I am in the profession I am today because my mother cultivated in me a love and respect for books.

When I became a mother thirteen years ago, I found myself following in my mother's footsteps. As my daughter sat quietly in her baby seat, or as we snuggled in the rocking chair, I read her the stories of *Goodnight Moon*, *Pat the Bunny*, and *Mother Goose*. She was far too young to understand the stories, but I knew the impact of reading to a child.

And I was right.

Just as my mother was.

Today, as a teenager, my daughter loves to read. I often find her hidden away in her room with a new (or old) book she has discovered, just like her mother used to do.

And I am thankful. Thankful for a daughter who reads, thankful for a life rich with books, and thankful for a mother who did all that she could to encourage my love affair with reading.

Angela Elwell Hunt is the award-winning and best-selling author of more than fifty books, including *The Tale of Three Trees*, published by Lion, and *Dreamers*, published by Bethany House. Her mother, Frankie Elwell, was a telephone operator who is now retired. Mrs. Elwell spends her days in Rockledge, Florida, where she sings in a choir and is active in her church. Each Thanksgiving, Angela, her mother and the extended family rent a banquet hall for a special get together. It is a time that both of them treasure.

Chapter Forty-nine

A LIVING LULLABY

by Ellen Gunderson Traylor

If "Carol" means song, my mother, Carol Gunderson, is a living lullaby.

A lullaby gives comfort and assurance to a child. It induces sleep, filling the childish spirit with pleasant images and a contented rhythm.

But its effects do not apply only to sleep and dreams. A lullaby can carry over into the daytime, charging the creative hours with hope and joy.

Though my mother is not a singer, if I were to sum up her essence in one word, that word would be "contentment"—the kind of contentment that a pleasant song, a lullaby, can express.

It is that essence of contentment that typifies her approach to motherhood, and her day-to-day dealings with the challenges of existence.

My mother's life has not always been easy.

She has admitted to me, from time to time, that she felt unwanted as a child. Probably a "surprise" to her middle-aged parents, she followed in the shadow of a dynamic sister who was thirteen years her senior; she sometimes felt that she was an interference or a burden.

Though she knew that her mother loved her, there was little expression of the fact on that Victorian mother's part. When Mother was only eleven, her mother died of cancer, and she was raised by a lonely and withdrawn father and his widowed sister on a small ranch in California.

I have often imagined my mother riding over the rolling hills of her Pajaro Valley acreage, with the horse who was her best friend and confidant. Mother recounts more than once that she shared her deepest yearnings and her adolescent dreams with that horse, in lieu of the mother who was not there.

As a young girl, Mother determined that any child she had would know it was loved, and that she would see to it that any son or daughter of hers grew up feeling valued.

This she accomplished.

When I was small, Mother would call me to her at unexpected moments, pull me onto her lap and say, "We're going to hug and squeeze." And then we would wrap our arms about each other and squeeze until we were almost breathless.

"Hug and squeeze" was a private game, requiring no words, but it was an absolute physical assurance of love.

As it turned out, I was my parents' only child. This was not by choice. My mother miscarried several times as I was growing up. I therefore had her full attention, but I have no doubt that she would have exhibited the same devotion to any number of children who had the privilege of being her offspring.

Mother's purposeful reinforcement of my sense of worth came long before "the child's need for self-esteem" became a parenting maxim. No one needed to tell Mother that children must feel valued.

I could give a long list of the ways in which my mother has been there for me. She was not much of a socializer, being the "quiet song" that she is. But she went out of her way to make special events out of my birthdays, my holidays, and my teenage milestones, baking special cakes and helping me decorate the house for all sorts of childhood gatherings. She bore with me through the agony of piano lessons, an instrument she had mastered but which was an ivory-toothed mystery to me. When my total lack of musical ability became painfully evident, she was wise enough to let me give up. She likewise bore with me through the torture of mathematics and science, which were the bane of my school years. When I brought home low grades in these subjects, she said little, only focusing on the A's and B's of my "right brain" achievements.

When she saw in me an area of true talent, she encouraged it as if it were her own.

When I was only ten, my mother published my first book.

I wrote the story, she typed it and illustrated it. It is the story of a ten-year-old backwoods boy. There is exactly one copy of *Rodney* in existence, but as much care went into its publication as has gone into any of the fourteen I have written since.

To this day, my parents are always the first to read my manuscripts. It is an unwritten rule that they are my primary editors, and if they had been paid for the hours of consultation they have provided throughout my writing career, they might be wealthy.

My mother could have been anything she wanted to be. A beautiful, statuesque girl, with deep auburn hair and a graceful carriage, she loved to dance. She was raised until age eleven by a strict mother who believed dancing was worldy and ungodly. When she accepted Christ as a teenager, she believed she must give up dancing, and so she did, as an act of devotion.

She could have gone on to be a teacher or a businesswoman. She was top graduate from Watsonville High School, and she is still a very bright lady. She has a head for numbers and has been a bookkeeper and librarian. But my mother's first love has always been her home and family, and her ultimate contentment has been homemaking. I often wish I had inherited mom's housekeeping ability, and her joy of sewing, cooking, and the "womanly arts." Those talents have generally eluded me. I take more after my father, being more outgoing and "ambitious" in the public sense. But, I do credit the greatest gift of my womanhood to my mother: a sense of inner directedness that finds its root in faith.

My mother taught me about Jesus from the time I could understand anything. I do not recall a time that I did not know who he was or what he was about. On the end pages of my mother's Bible are large scrawls in green crayon, which I made in some moment of childish creativity. I guess I began my career as a "biblical" writer at that time.

Mother's Bible has always been her primary reading matter and the beloved book was a fixture in our house—lying on her night stand, on the dining room table or beside her chair in the living room. It is underlined throughout, with notes in the margins, a chronicle of more than fifty years of Christian walk. Alongside Mother's Bible there have always been commentaries and devotionals, and shelves of Bible history, archeology, and Christian classics.

Some of my most vivid memories of my mother relate to when I would go out on dates as a teenager. I would poke my head in the living room to say good-bye; she would be sitting in her chair, the Bible resting quietly beside her. With no verbal instruction whatsoever, she impressed her expectations upon me.

My mother perfectly fits the description that Peter gives of a virtuous woman: "And let not your adornment be external only—braiding the hair, and wearing gold jewelry, and putting on dresses; but let it be the hidden person of the heart, with the imperishable quality of a gentle and quiet spirit, which is precious in the sight of God. For in this way in former times the holy women also, who hoped in God, used to adorn themselves..." (1 Peter 3:3-5a NASB).

The meekness of which Peter speaks is not weakness. My mother, who has rarely raised her voice and who has never put herself in the public eye, is nonetheless a strong and confident woman. "Meekness" in the Greek means "strength in restraint."

Such is the contentment and faith that is my mother's.

She is a "song" of strength and joy to all who know her. And she is her daughter's best friend.

Ellen Gunderson Traylor is a well-loved Christian author of fifteen books; the most recent is *Jerusalem—The City of God*. When Ellen is not writing, she is at the Christian bookstore she owns in Polson, Montana. Ellen and her mother, Amelia Carol Gunderson, enjoy vacationing together on the Oregon Coast.